Requirements Engineering

Elizabeth Hull • Ken Jackson
Jeremy Dick

Requirements Engineering

 Springer

Elizabeth Hull, BSc, PhD, CEng, FBCS
School of Computing and Mathematics
University of Ulster
Newtownabbey, Co Antrim
UK
mec.hull@ulst.ac.uk

Jeremy Dick, BSc (Eng), ACGI,
DPhil, DIC, MA
Integrate Systems Engineering Ltd
Bath
UK
jeremy.dick@integrate.biz

Ken Jackson, BSc, MSc, MBCS
University of Ulster
Newtownabbey, Co Antrim
UK
kenjackson@fastmail.fm

ISBN 978-1-84996-404-3   e-ISBN 978-1-84996-405-0
DOI 10.1007/978-1-84996-405-0
Springer London Dordrecht Heidelberg New York

British Library Cataloguing in Publication Data
A catalogue record for this book is available from the British Library

Library of Congress Control Number: 2010937427

Printed on acid-free paper

Springer is part of Springer Science+Business Media (www.springer.com)

We would like to dedicate this book as follows:

To my late parents John and Edna Hull

Elizabeth Hull

To my wife Chris,
To my children and their spouses Kate, Stef,
Andy, Amy and Pete
and to my grand children Lizzie, Alice, Emily
and Annabel

Ken Jackson

To my wife
Yvonne and to my children
Sebastian, Timothy, Angus, Robin and Felicity

Jeremy Dick

Preface to the Third Edition

In our desire to keep the material in this book current, the main driver in creating a new edition has been to adapt to the latest release of DOORS. Since the publication of Edition 2, Telelogic – the developer of DOORS – has been acquired by IBM, and the tool has become part of the IBM/Rational stable. While the basic functions of the tool remain unchanged, the look-and-feel has advanced considerably. Therefore, Chapter 9 has been updated for DOORS version 9.2.

At the same time, we felt the need to provide a more explicit definition of Requirements Engineering. In searching the literature, we could not find a satisfactory definition, and we have addressed this in Chapter 1.

Apart from this, there is an expanded description of Product Family Management in Chapter 8, and a variety of small corrections throughout.

We hope our readers – students and practitioners – continue to find this a valuable text in advancing their understanding of the topic.

April 2010

Elizabeth Hull
Ken Jackson
Jeremy Dick

Preface to the Second Edition

This second edition follows quickly on the first edition and is an indication of how fast the subject is changing and developing. In the past 2 years there have been significant advances and these are reflected in this new edition.

Essentially, this is an update that places more emphasis on modelling by describing a greater range of approaches to system modelling. It introduces the UML2, which is the recent standard approved by the OMG. There is also an enhanced discussion on the relationship between requirements management and modelling, which relates well to the concept of rich traceability.

The chapter on the requirements management tool DOORS has been revised to use Version 7 of the tool and this is complemented with examples taken from the DOORS/Analyst tool which demonstrates how the concepts of modelling can be captured and created within DOORS.

The text is still aimed at students and practitioners of systems engineering who are keen to gain knowledge of using requirements engineering for system development.

As before, a website supporting additional material is available at:
http://www.requirementsengineering.info

June 2004

Elizabeth Hull
Ken Jackson
Jeremy Dick

Preface to the First Edition

Requirements Engineering is common sense, but it is perceived to be difficult and is not well understood. For these reasons it is generally not very well done. The ever-increasing pressures on an organisation are often given as the main reasons for not introducing a more disciplined approach to requirements engineering, but its aim will be to do the job properly, so the task of the requirements engineer is to work out how best to help the organisation achieve its goal.

Systems engineering is critical in today's industry and requirements engineering is an important stage of that overall process. A good process is key to requirements engineering – it determines how efficiently and rapidly products can be generated. This is particularly important in a global competitive market where the 'time to market' and meeting stakeholder requirements are the key success factors.

Requirements engineering is also about management and hence issues in relation to requirements and management blend to show how requirements can be used to manage systems development.

The book is concerned with engineering requirements and how systems engineers may be helped to create better requirements. A generic process is presented which assists the reader in gaining a good understanding of the essence of requirements engineering. The process is then instantiated for the problem and solution domains of development. The book also addresses the concept of system modelling and presents various techniques and methods which are widely used. An important feature of the book is the presentation of approaches to traceability, the way in which it is captured and discusses metrics which can be derived from traceability. Finally the book presents an overview of DOORS which is a tool for requirements management. A case study is used to illustrate the process presented in the book and the features of the tool.

This book should be read by those systems engineers (requirements engineers) in industry, who, being practitioners are keen to gain knowledge of using requirements engineering for system development. The book will also be of interest to final year undergraduate students in Computer Science, Software Engineering and Systems Engineering studying a course in Requirements Engineering and also to postgraduate research students in Computer Science or more generally in Engineering.

The approach taken in the book is based on current research in Requirements Engineering, however it has not only taken the academic view but has also built substantially on current experience of working in industry to enable system engineers to manage requirements (and projects) more successfully. It provides a snapshot, in this rapidly evolving subject, of what we see as best practice in Requirements Engineering today.

A web site supporting additional material for the book can be found at: http:// www.requirementsengineering.info/

May 2002   Elizabeth Hull
                                                                      Ken Jackson
                                                                      Jeremy Dick

Acknowledgements

Thanks are due to a number of individuals and organisations who helped in various ways:

Richard Stevens, who inspired us with his work on requirements management and who laid the foundation for the work in this book. He was a founder of Requirements Engineering Ltd. (later Quality Systems and Software Ltd.), which developed the DOORS tool.

Les Oliver (who worked for Astrium at the time) for assistance in the development of statecharts for agreement, qualification and satisfaction.

Praxis Critical Systems (now Altran Praxis) for the initial concept of design justification which become *Rich Traceability*.

Keith Collyer, Jill Burnett and other colleagues of Telelogic Ltd. for contributions to ideas presented in this book and for reviews, comments, suggestions and encouragement.

Contents

Chapter 1
Introduction

There is no fair wind for one who knows not whither he is bound.

Lucius Annaeus Seneca, philosopher, 3–65 AD

1.1 Introduction to Requirements

If ever systems development projects needed a "fair wind", they certainly do so today. Fast-changing technology and increased competition are placing ever-increasing pressure on the development process. Effective requirements engineering lies at the heart of an organisation's ability to guide the ship and to keep pace with the rising tide of complexity.

Software is currently the dominant force of change of new products. The trend is driven by three key factors:

Arbitrary complexity. The most complex systems tend to be those with software, often integrated deep inside the system's components. The complexity of such products is limited only by the imagination of those who *conceive them.*

Instant distribution. Today a company can think of a new product, implement it in software, and rapidly distribute it around the world. For example, a car manu-facturer can improve the software in its diagnostic system, and then transmit it electronically around the world to tens of thousands of car showrooms in a day.

"Off-the-shelf" components. Systems are now constructed from bought-in technology and ready-made components with a corresponding reduction in the product development cycle.

The net impact of these trends is a sudden intensity of competition, and the ability to monopolise the rewards from the new technology without needing large factories. The result is pressure to reduce the development cycle and the time to deploy technology. But 'time to market' is not sufficient. The real goal is 'time to market with the right product'. Establishing the requirements enables us to agree on and visualise the 'right product'. A vital part of the systems engineering process, requirements engineering first

E. Hull et al., *Requirements Engineering*, DOI 10.1007/978-1-84996-405-0_1,
© Springer-Verlag London Limited 2011

defines the problem scope and then links all subsequent development information to it. Only in this way can one expect to control and direct project activity; managing the development of a solution that is both appropriate and cost-effective.

Requirements are the basis for every project, defining what the stakeholders – users, customers, suppliers, developers, businesses – in a potential new system need from it, and also what the system must do in order to satisfy that need. To be well understood by everybody they are generally expressed in natural language and herein lies the challenge: to capture the need or problem completely and unambiguously without resorting to specialist jargon or conventions. Once communicated and agreed, requirements drive the project activity. However the needs of the stakeholders may be many and varied, and may indeed conflict. These needs may not be clearly defined at the start, may be constrained by factors outside their control or may be influenced by other goals which themselves change in the course of time. Without a relatively stable requirements base a development project can only flounder. It is like setting off on a sea journey without any idea of the destination and with no navigation chart. Requirements provide both the "navigation chart" and the means of steering towards the selected destination.

Agreed requirements provide the basis for planning the development of a system and accepting it on completion. They are essential when sensible and informed tradeoffs have to be made and they are also vital when, as inevitably happens, changes are called for during the development process. How can the impact of a change be assessed without an adequately detailed model of the prior system? Otherwise what is there to revert to if the change needs to be unwound?

Even as the problem to be solved and potential solutions are defined one must assess the risks of failing to provide a satisfactory solution. Few sponsors or stakeholders will support product or systems development without a convincing risk management strategy. Requirements enable the management of risks from the earliest possible point in development. Risks raised against requirements can be tracked, their impact assessed, and the effects of mitigation and fallback plans understood, long before substantial development costs have been incurred.

Requirements therefore form the basis for:

- Project planning
- Risk management
- Acceptance testing
- Trade off
- Change control

The most common reasons for project failures are not technical and Table 1.1 identifies the main reasons why projects fail. The data is drawn from surveys conducted by the Standish Group in 1995 and 1996, and shows the percentage of projects that stated various reasons for project failure. Those marked with an asterisk are directly related to requirements.

The problems fall into three main categories:

Requirements – either poorly organised, poorly expressed, weakly related to stakeholders, changing too rapidly, or unnecessary; unrealistic expectations

Table 1.1 Reasons for project failure

* Incomplete requirements	13.1%
* Lack of user involvement	12.4%
Lack of resources	10.6%
* Unrealistic expectations	9.9%
Lack of executive support	9.3%
* Changing requirements/specifications	8.7%
Lack of planning	8.1%
* Didn't need it any longer	7.5%

Standish Group 1995 & 1996
Scientific American, Sept. 1994

Table 1.2 Project success factors

* User involvement	15.9%
Management support	13.9%
* Clear statement of requirements	13.0%
Proper planning	9.6%
* Realistic expectations	8.2%
Smaller milestones	7.7%
Competent staff	7.2%
* Ownership	5.3%

Standish Group 1995 & 1996
Scientific American, Sept. 1994

Management problems of resources – failure to have enough money, and lack of support, or failure to impose proper discipline and planning, many of these arise from poor requirements control
Politics – which contributes to the first two problems

All these factors can be addressed at fairly low cost.

Project success factors are not quite the inverse of the failure factors, but as can be seen in Table 1.2, Management support and proper planning are clearly seen as important here – the larger the project, and the longer its schedule, the higher the chance of failure (Scientific American, Sept. 1994).

This book considers an engineering approach to requirements in general and requirements management in particular. It explains the differences between stakeholder requirements and system requirements and indicates how requirements can be used to manage system development. It also shows how traceability from stakeholder requirements through system requirements to design can be used to measure progress, manage change and assess risks. It exposes the reader to those qualities of requirements that make them suitable for validating and verifying designs and solutions, and stresses the need to produce designs that can be integrated and tested easily.

Requirements management has important interfaces to project management, which is recognised in the book through the presence of Chapter 8, "Management Aspects of Requirements Engineering".

1.2   Introduction to Systems Engineering

This book is not just about requirements for software. The principles and practice of requirements engineering apply to complete systems in which software may only play a small part.

For example, consider a railway system such as the West Coast Mainline from London to Glasgow. A high-level requirement on the system may be to achieve a journey time from Euston Station in London to Glasgow in Scotland in less than 250 min. Satisfaction of this single requirement arises from the coordinated interaction of every major component of the system:

- The trains, and their speed
- The tracks, and their ability to support high-speed trains
- The stations and station staff, and the waiting time they impose on the trains
- The drivers, and their ability to control the trains
- The signalling subsystems
- The train control and detection subsystems
- The power delivery subsystems

While the software in the signalling and control subsystems plays a vital part in achieving this requirement, it cannot deliver alone. The complete solution involves the whole system. In fact, most requirements are satisfied by the properties that emerge from the way the system as a whole behaves.

What then is meant by a "system"?

> *System*: a collection of components – machine, software and human – which co-operate in an organised way to achieve some desired result – the requirements.

Thus systems include people. In the West Coast Mainline, the drivers and station staff – the training they receive and the procedures they use – are just as important as the software and machine components.

Since components must co-operate, interfaces between components are a vital consideration in system (and requirements) engineering – interfaces between people and machine components, between machine components, and between software components. An example of a machine-to-machine interface in a railway system is the way train wheels interface with the track. Apart from the physical arrangements (which are designed to allow the train to be guided along the track without sliding off), electrical currents across the rails may be used to detect the presence of the train as part of the train control subsystem.

At the heart of the concept of a "system", lies the idea of "emergent properties". This refers to the fact that the usefulness of a system does not depend on any particular part of the system, but emerges from the way in which its components interact. Emergent properties may be desirable, in that they have been anticipated and designed into the system so as to make the system useful; or they may be undesirable, in other words unanticipated side effects, such as harm to the environment. The trick in system engineering is to be able to harness desirable emergent properties, and avoid the undesirable ones.

Another important concept is that of "systems of systems". Every system can be construed as being part of a larger, enclosing system. For example, the West Coast Mainline is part of a wider railway system, and intersects with other major and minor routes. The entire railway system is part of the wider transport system, and interacts in all kinds of ways with the road and air transport networks. The transport system itself provides essential infrastructure for the transport of goods and people as part of the economy of the country. And the country is part of the wider world, and so forth.

To understand the requirements of a system properly is to understand its enclosing system. Often the correct functioning of a system depends on provisions of the enclosing system. For example, the ability of a helicopter to fly depends on the environment provided by the earth, its gravitation field and atmosphere.

Take another, very simple, example: a cup (Fig. 1.1). It is evident that it has components: a handle and a bowl-shaped container. What purpose do these components serve? The bowl is for containing liquid, and the handle is to allow the bowl to be held by someone without getting burnt. One may deduce that the purpose of – or requirement – for the cup is to allow a human being to transfer hot liquid into the mouth without spilling it or getting burnt.

The cup is rich in interfaces. It can be placed on a flat surface for stability; it can be held in a human hand; it can be filled with fluid and emptied; it must interface with the fluid for sustained containment; and it must deliver fluid to the human mouth.

But there are other observations to be made:

- The cup is no good on its own. It depends on the motor-movement of the human arm to achieve its purpose.
- The bowl part of the cup depends crucially on the presence of gravity for its correct functioning. It also has to be used correctly: holding the cup upside down would cause spilling, and may cause scalding.

At the end of the day, the ability of this simple cup to fulfil its purpose depends on:

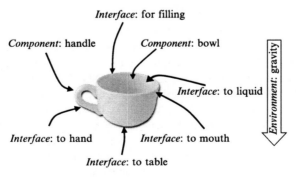

Fig. 1.1 A cup as a very simple system

- The properties that emerge from the interaction of its components
- Appropriate interfaces to external components
- Its correct embedding in the enclosing system – being held in the human hand and lifted by the arm
- The presence of the proper environment – another solution would be necessary in weightless conditions

In summary, the engineering of requirements must take the nature of systems into account. Essential considerations are emergent properties, the constraints and provisions of the external environment, and the interfaces with surrounding systems.

1.3   Defining Requirements Engineering

Because of the inter-connectedness of requirements with other aspects of systems engineering and project management, it is quite challenging to find a satisfactory scope for a definition of requirements engineering.

1.3.1   Definition of a Requirement

First of all, what is meant by a requirement? Here is a typical definition drawn from IEEE-STD-1220-1998 (IEEE 1998):

> *Requirement*: a statement that identifies a product or process operational, functional, or design characteristic or constraint, which is unambiguous, testable or measurable, and necessary for product or process acceptability (by consumers or internal quality assurance guidelines).

This definition draws out a number of facets of a requirement that are briefly discussed here, and in greater detail later:

- *Statement*. That a requirement should be a statement is perhaps biased towards textual expression, whereas they can also be captured in tabular form, such as in Tom Gilb's Planguage (Gilb 2005), in diagrammatic form in notations such as UML (OMG 2003), in formal notations, such as Z (Spivey 1989), VDM (Jones 1986), LOTOS (Bjorner 1987) and the B-Method (Abrial 1996), or in domain-specific notations, e.g. (Chaochen, Z; Hoare, C.A.R.; Ravn, A.P. 1991). The important concept, though, is to have a set of traceable, manageable elements identified as requirements.
- *Product or process*. Complete solutions contain varying mixtures of product (things that are built in response to requirements) and process (procedures for using the things that are built). Requirements may therefore define process as well as product. In addition to this, there may be requirements that stipulate how the product should be developed, usually for quality control purposes.

- *Operational, functional, or design characteristic or constraint.* There are many different kinds of requirement, giving rise to different kinds of language, analysis, modelling, process and solution. Note that this definition has carefully avoided the term "non-functional", since there is heated debate about what this actually means. Design characteristics cover performance, usability, safety, maintainability and a host of other qualities.
- *Unambiguous.* A statement of requirement has desirable qualities that will be addressed in detail later. In brief, a requirement should lend itself to a clear, single understanding, common to all parties involved.
- *Testable or measurable.* Requirements are used to test that the design or solution is acceptable. For this to be possible, the requirement should be quantified, thus providing a means of "measuring" the solution against it.
- *Necessary for product or process acceptability.* This highlights the multi-dimensional role that requirements play: they serve to define what should be designed and developed, and also define how the solution should be tested and accepted. They have an influence in the earliest stages of the development process as well as in the latest stages during acceptance.
- *By consumers or internal quality assurance guidelines.* Requirements come from many sources, including but not limited to customers, regulatory bodies, users and internal quality procedures.

Some other synonyms for requirements are: aims, aspirations, capabilities, criteria, constraints, directives, doctrines, duties, expectations, features, functions, goals, missions, needs, obligations, objectives, orders, regulations, rules, etc.

1.3.2 Definition of a Stakeholder

The term "stakeholder" has already been used without giving a definition:

Stakeholder: An individual, group of people, organisation or other entity that has a direct or indirect interest (or stake) in a system.

A stakeholder's interest in a system may arise from *using* the system, *benefiting* from the system (in terms of revenue or other advantage), *being disadvantaged* by the system (in terms, for instance, of cost or potential harm), *being responsible* for the system, or otherwise *being affected* by it.

Stakeholders are legitimate sources of requirements.

1.3.3 Definition of Requirements Engineering

The term "requirements engineering" is often too narrowly equated with requirements analysis, which is just one of the activities within the wider discipline. The emphasis on engineering is useful for two main reasons:

1. Dealing with requirements is an essential part of every engineering endeavour. Indeed, requirements engineering is a subset of systems engineering in general, not just software engineering.
2. The term subsumes the wide variety of other titles given to activities relating to requirements, such as requirements analysis and the two terms used for key process areas in CMMI® (CarnegieMellon 2006): requirements management and requirements development.

The following, broader definition is one of the most long-standing, and comes from a DoD software strategy document dated 1991:

> Requirements engineering "involves all life-cycle activities devoted to identification of user requirements, analysis of the requirements to derive additional requirements, documentation of the requirements as a specification, and validation of the documented requirements against user needs, as well as processes that support these activities" (DoD 1991).

While this definition covers the identification, analysis, development and validation of requirements, it omits to mention the vital role that requirements play in accepting and verifying the solution (usually called verification rather than validation.) A more recent definition, given in the context of software engineering, suffers the same defect, but emphasizes the goal-oriented (or purpose-oriented) nature of requirements engineering, and hints at the importance of understanding and documenting the relationships between requirements and other development artefacts:

> Requirements engineering is the branch of software engineering concerned with the real-world goals for, functions of, and constraints on software systems. It is also concerned with the relationship of these factors to precise specifications of software behavior, and to their evolution over time and across software families (Zave 1997).

For the purposes of this book, the following definition will be used:

Requirements engineering: the subset of systems engineering concerned with discovering, developing, tracing, analyzing, qualifying, communicating and managing requirements that define the system at successive levels of abstraction.

This definition lists carefully selected key activities that are considered proper to requirements engineering. There are some activities closely related to requirements that are considered to be part of some other discipline. An example of this is system testing or verification; while requirements should have the qualities necessary to allow the solution to be verified, the verification activity itself is another discipline. It also references the concept of requirements existing at multiple levels of development.

Here are some notes on the definition:

- *Discovering.* This covers a number of terms often used, such as requirements elicitation and capture.
- *Tracing.* Tracing of requirements to other artefacts, including requirements at other layers, provides a means of validating requirements against real-world

needs, of capturing rationale for the design, and of verifying the design against requirements.

- *Qualifying.* This refers to all kinds of testing activity, covering testing of the design and solution, including unit, component, integration, system, acceptance testing. There is considerable disagreement over the meaning of the terms "verification" and "validation". The term "qualifying" is preferred, because it is about ensuring that the solution has the required "qualities." In so much as the terms are used in this book, to validate requirements is to check a formal expression of requirements against informal needs as understood in the minds of stakeholders, and to verify requirements is to check their internal consistency within layers and between layers of abstraction.
- *Communicating.* Requirements are the means of communication through which customers, suppliers, developers, users and regulators can agree on what is to be achieved.
- *Levels of abstraction.* This makes reference to the practice of organizing requirements into layers and of tracing the satisfaction relationship between those layers. The requirements of the top layer define the system in terms of the problems to be solved as agreed by the stakeholders and validated against their real needs; requirements at subsequent layers define the whole or part of the system in terms of an implementable solution as verified against the requirements at the layer above; requirements at every layer provide a precise means of qualifying the solution. Some people refer to the relationship between requirements induced by recording satisfaction between layers as a requirements hierarchy, but in reality the many-to-many relationship forms a graph or heterarchy.

1.4 Requirements and Quality

The consequences of having no requirements are many and varied. There is ample evidence around us of systems that failed because requirements were not properly organised. However well the system may appear to work at first, if it is not the system that users want or need then it will be useless – or user-less.

It is interesting to consider the relationship between requirements and quality. The term "quality" may be understood in a variety of ways. When asked about quality cars, one might mention Rolls Royce, Mercedes or Jaguar. This inherent confusion between "quality" and "luxury" is exposed if consideration is given to choosing the best car for the annual RAC rally. Neither Rolls Royce, Mercedes nor Jaguar is chosen, since none of them exhibit the right weight/power ratio, ground clearance and robustness properties. Recent history shows that the best quality car in its class is a Skoda – not a luxury car, but the right quality of car for the job.

Quality, then, is "fitness for purpose" or conformance to requirements – it is providing something that satisfies the customer and in doing so ensures that the needs of all the stakeholders are taken into account.

As is seen in Chapter 8, requirements engineering acts as a compliment to other management considerations, such as cost and schedule, by providing a vital focus on the delivery of quality. Every management decision is a compromise between cost, schedule and quality, three inter-related axes.

Since requirements engineering is a discipline that applies from the start of the development lifecycle, the leverage on quality that can be exercised by proper requirements management is proportionately greater. Relatively little effort expended in early stages of development can reap dividends in the later stages. The adage "Quality is Free" (the title of a book by Phil Crosby) holds true, in that getting it right at the outset can save huge amounts of effort that would have been necessary to put things right later. Improving requirements means improving the quality of the product.

1.5 Requirements and the Lifecycle

There is a common misconception that requirements engineering is just a single phase that is carried out and completed at the outset of product development. The purpose of this section is to demonstrate that requirements engineering has a vital role to play at every stage of development.

As an initial approach, consider one of the very last activities in the development process: acceptance testing. What is a system accepted against? The stakeholder requirements. So it can be seen straight away that requirements developed at the outset are still in use in the final stages of development.

The classic V-Model, which is used to portray the various stages of development, has its basis in this relationship between testing and requirements. Figure 1.2 shows this relationship at every stage of development.

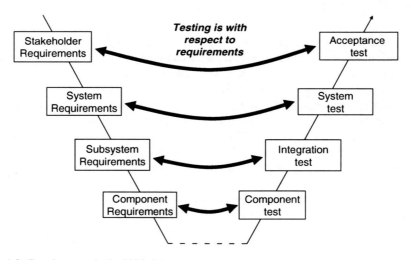

Fig. 1.2 Requirements in the V-Model

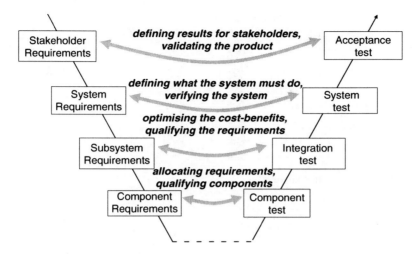

Fig. 1.3 Requirements engineering in layers

The V-Model also views development in terms of layers, each layer addressing the concerns proper to the corresponding stage of development. Although slightly different processes may be used at each layer, the basic pattern of requirements use is the same – a point reinforced through the introduction of a generic process in Chapter 2. Figure 1.3 shows the main concern of requirements engineering at each layer.

Another role that requirements can play in an organisation is to act as a means of communicating between projects. This is a good idea, because many organisations wish to:

- Maximise reuse of artefacts across projects
- Manage families of similar products
- Use programme management to coordinate activities
- Optimise process by learning from the experiences of other projects

A good set of stakeholder requirements can provide a concise non-technical description of what is being developed at a level that is accessible to senior management. Similarly, the system requirements can form an excellent technical summary of a development project. These descriptions can serve as a basis for comparison with other activities. This is illustrated in Fig. 1.4.

If requirements are to play such a central role in systems development, they need to be maintained. To change the design of a product without having also updated the requirements to reflect that change, is to store up huge problems for later stages of development. Hence requirements engineering connects strongly with change management.

Whether change originates from within a project – e.g. technical issues arising from details of the design – or from without – e.g. evolving stakeholder needs – the impact of that change on quality, cost and schedule needs to be assessed. This assessment forms the basis on which to:

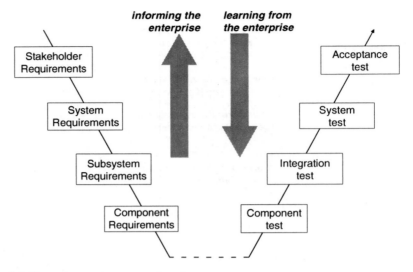

Fig. 1.4 Enterprise requirements engineering

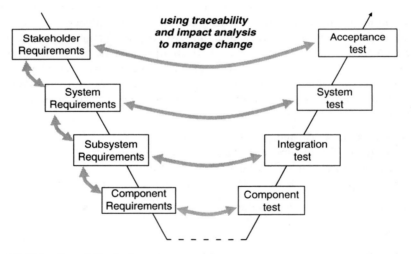

Fig. 1.5 Role of tracebility in change management

- Accept or reject the change (where that is a choice)
- Negotiate the cost of the change with the customer/suppliers
- Organise the redevelopment work

The key concept that enables this kind of impact analysis is requirements tracing, a topic treated in greater detail in Section 1.6, and in Chapters 2 and 7. Suffice to say that change management is an integral part of the requirements engineering process. This role is illustrated in Fig. 1.5.

Quite apart from change management, a manager's ability to control a project is considerably enhanced by good requirements engineering. Without requirements, project managers have no means of gauging how well the project is going, or even if it is going in the right direction. When it comes to changes there is nothing against which change can be judged. What is more, when they do come to intervene, their only approach is at a technical level, which is inappropriate to their role, and which interferes with the technical role properly played by the engineers. Requirements well expressed at the appropriate level give managers just the right view of the project to be able to perform their role.

In summary, requirements are essential to the health of every system development. They influence the whole development from beginning to end and from top to bottom. Without effective requirements engineering, development projects are like ships drifting rudderless in a storm! Above all else, with good requirements management, hearing the voice of the users and customers ceases to be a game of Chinese whispers, and becomes a matter of clear lines of communication throughout the development process.

1.6   Requirements Tracing

In the requirements engineering context, tracing is about understanding how high-level requirements – objectives, goals, aims, aspirations, expectations, needs – are transformed into low-level requirements. It is therefore primarily concerned with the relationships between layers of information.

In a business context, one may be interested in how

- Business vision *is interpreted as*
- Business objectives *are implemented as*
- Business organisation and processes

In an engineering context, the interest may focus on how

- Stakeholder requirements *are met by*
- System requirements *are partitioned into*
- Subsystems *are implemented as*
- Components

Tracing can contribute to the following benefits:

Greater confidence in meeting objectives. Establishing and formalising relationships engenders greater reflection on how objectives are satisfied.
Ability to assess the impact of change. Various forms of impact analysis become possible in the presence of tracing.
Improved accountability of subordinate organisations. Greater clarity in how suppliers contribute to the whole.
Ability to track progress. It is notoriously difficult to measure progress when all that you are doing is creating and revising documents. Processes surrounding tracing allow precise measures of progress in the early stages.
Ability to balance cost against benefit. Relating product components to the requirements allows benefit to be assessed against cost.

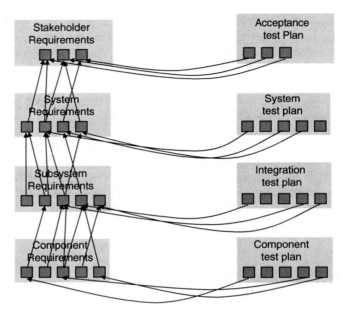

Fig. 1.6 Requirements tracing

Traceability relationships are usually many-to-many – that is, one lower-level requirement may be linked to several higher-level ones, and vice versa. The simplest way to implement tracing is to link requirements statements in one layer with statements in another. Requirements management tools typically allow such linking by drag-and-drop between paragraphs of documents. The links are rather like hyperlinks in web pages, but should ideally be traversable in either direction. Figure 1.6 shows tracing downwards through the layers of requirements, and across to the test information.

The direction of the arrows follows a particular convention: information traces back to the information it responds to. There are a number of reasons for this convention:

- It usually corresponds to the chronological order in which information is created: always link back to the older information.
- It usually corresponds to access rights due to ownership: one owns the outgoing links from a document, someone else owns the incoming links.

Various forms of traceability analysis can be used to support requirements engineering processes, presented in Table 1.3.

When performing coverage analysis, it is important to realise that counting links tells only a small part of the story. The presence of one or more links gives no indication that the coverage provides correct or complete satisfaction, which must

Table 1.3 Types of traceability analysis

Type of analysis	Description	Processes supported
Impact analysis	Following incoming links, in answer to the question: "What if this was to change?"	Change management
Derivation analysis	Following outgoing links, in answer to the question: "Why is this here?"	Cost/benefit analysis
Coverage analysis	Counting statements that have links, in answer to the question: "Have I covered everything?" (May be used as an approximate measure of progress, but not of sufficiency – see below.)	General engineering Management reporting

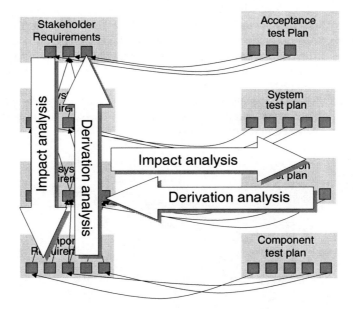

Fig. 1.7 Impact and derivation analysis

remain an engineering judgement. We will see later that two aspects have to be considered when assessing the quality of tracing: sufficiency and necessity.

Impact analysis is used to determine what other artefacts in the development might be affected if a selected artefact changes. This is illustrated in Fig. 1.7. The impact is potential; creative analysis has to be carried out by an engineer to determine the exact nature of the impact, if any.

Derivation analysis works in the opposite direction to impact analysis. A low level artefact – such as a requirement, design element or test – is selected, and the tracing is used to determine what higher-level requirements have given rise to it. Elements in the design that do not so trace back are potentially adding cost without benefit.

Finally, coverage analysis can be used to determine that all requirements do trace downwards to lower layers, and across to tests. The absence of such a trace is a fairly certain indication that the requirement will not be met or tested. The presence of a link does not, of course, ensure that the requirement *will* be met – that again requires creative engineering judgement.

Coverage can also be used as a measure of progress: how far have the systems engineers got in responding to the stakeholder requirements? Suppose the task of writing systems requirements in response to stakeholder requirements is given to an engineer. As she writes system requirements, she links them back to the stakeholder requirements she is responding to. (By doing it as she goes along, the insertion of tracing is very little extra overhead – it is much more difficult to establish tracing after both documents have been written!)

At any stage of the task, the engineers' progress can be measured in terms of the percentage of stakeholder requirements that have been covered so far. This is a very useful management tool during the early stages of development.

The same principle can be used to measure progress in planning tests. What percentage of the requirements have tests defined so far? These two dimensions of coverage are summarized in Fig. 1.8.

Because of the kinds of analysis that can be carried out, tracing is a simple concept that lies at the heart of the requirements engineering process. More advanced forms of tracing are discussed in detail in Chapter 7.

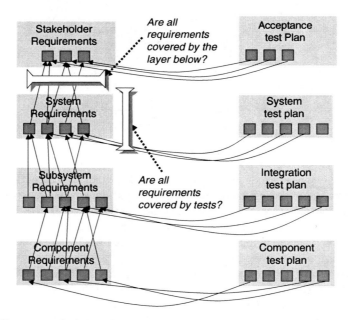

Fig. 1.8 Coverage analysis

1.7   Requirements and Modelling

It is important to understand the relationship between requirements management and system modelling. They are mutually supportive activities that should not be equated. Figure 1.9 compares the relationship to a sandwich. In this analogy, requirements management is the "bread and butter" of the development cycle. The "filling" provided by system modelling explains and exposes the analysis and design that has led to subsequent layers of requirements.

Some people talk about requirements modelling. This is a misnomer. You model the system design, not the requirements. Modelling supports the design activity, and is where most of the creative work takes place. It assists the engineer in understanding enough of the system to decompose the requirements at a particular level into the next level down. The requirements themselves are a complete snapshot of what is required at each level in increasing levels of detail.

A particular model never says everything about a system – if it did, it would not be a model. For this reason, several different, possibly inter-related, models of systems are often used to cover a variety of different aspects. It is left to the expression of requirements – usually in textual form – to cover those aspects not modelled.

A model is an abstraction of a system that deliberately focuses on some aspects of a system to the exclusion of others. Abstraction is, in this sense, avoidance of distraction – ignoring those details that, although important, are not relevant to a particular model. The advantage of this is that smaller amounts of related information can be collected, processed, organised and analysed, applying various specific techniques pertinent to the aspects under study.

Where a large amount of complex information has to be managed, modelling provides a means of zooming in, collecting together subsets of the data for a particular purpose, and zooming out once more to appreciate the whole. It aids in maintaining a system-wide grasp through focussing on small amounts of information at a time.

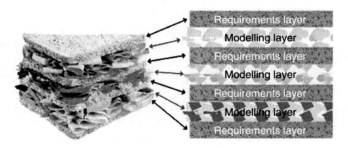

Fig. 1.9   The systems engineering sandwich

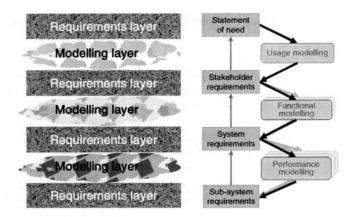

Fig. 1.10 Requirements and modeling

Figure 1.10 portrays the inter-related roles that requirements and system modelling play. Models assist the requirements engineer in analysing the requirements at a particular level so as to:

- Communicate with the customer, and improve mutual understanding of the system to be developed.
- Analyse the system to ascertain the presence of desired emergent properties (and the absence of undesirable ones).
- Determine how to satisfy the requirements by deriving new requirements at the layer below.

The nature of the models used will vary from layer to layer. At the top layer, usage models such as "stakeholder scenarios" are used to derive the first statement of stakeholder requirements. Following this, various kinds of functional model may be used to derive system requirements from the stakeholder requirements. For software, such models could include UML class diagrams, message sequence charts and state charts (see Chapter 3 for more details on these modelling techniques).

Moving from system requirements to architecture, the concerns become focused on various aspects of performance. Multiple models may be used to give confidence that the selected architecture can deliver against non-functional as well as functional requirements. Here, models may include queuing theory used to assess performance, wind tunnels for assessing aerodynamics, timetable modelling to assess viability of journey times.

As is evident from these examples, the nature of the models also varies from application to application. The modelling of timetables may be appropriate for the design of railway systems, but not for aircraft design, where the modelling of aerodynamics is rather more appropriate. (Aerodynamics may also be important to high-speed trains, of course.) Message sequence charts may be used in communications systems, but data-rich applications will find data-focused modelling such as entity-relationship diagramming more appropriate.

Whereas the models may vary, the principles of requirements management remain generic across applications. Since this book is about requirements engineering, it also covers the closely associated subject of modelling and methods.

1.8 Requirements and Testing

As has been discussed above, testing is closely related to requirements at every level. In its broadest sense, testing is any activity that allows defects in the system to be detected or prevented, where a defect is a departure from requirements. So testing activities include reviews, inspections, analysis through modelling as well as the classical tests of components, subsystem and systems that are carried out.

Because of the diversity of testing activities, the term *qualification* is used in this book to refer to all such activities.

Qualification should begin as early as possible, since waiting until the system is almost complete before carrying out any kind of testing can lead to very expensive design changes and rebuilds. The earliest kinds of qualification action take place during the design of the system, and include requirements reviews, design inspections, and various forms of analysis carried out on system models.

Figure 1.11 portrays the qualification strategy along a time-line below the V-Model. Early qualification actions relate to the left-hand side of the V-Model, later ones to the test stages on the right-hand side.

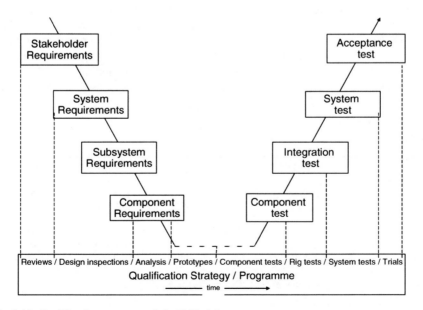

Fig. 1.11 Qualification strategy and the V-Model

A single stakeholder requirement will typically give rise to a multitude of qualification activities at various stages of development. Where a requirement is satisfied through useful emergent properties, qualification of components alone is insufficient; tests have to be carried out at the level where emergent properties are manifest.

1.9 Requirements in the Problem and Solution Domains

Systems engineering is concerned with developing and managing effective solutions to problems. As has been discussed, it is a staged process vital for businesses in enabling them to produce the right product within acceptable time-scales and costs.

Early in the process, the definition of the requirements for the product to be built is of prime importance. From a management and engineering point of view, a clear distinction should be made between the "problem domain" and the "solution domain". Those stages of development associated with the highest levels of system description – statement of need, usage modelling and stakeholder requirements – should be firmly rooted in the problem domain, whereas subsequent layers, starting with system requirements, operate in the solution domain.

Table 1.4 portrays the ideal boundary between the problem and solution domains, and the roles that the top requirements layers play.

There is an important principle of abstraction at play here. The initial statement of capability should state no more than is necessary to define the problem, and avoid any reference to particular solutions. This allows freedom to the system engineers to carry out their role, which is to devise the best solution without preconceived ideas.

Modelling assists in the derivation of the next layer of requirements, and tends to consider possible solutions, even at a high level. To avoid inappropriate solution bias, rather than focus on the system in question, early modelling should focus on the immediately *enclosing* system. For instance, if a radio system is being developed

Table 1.4 Problem and solution spaces

Requirements layer	Domain	View	Role
Stakeholder requirements	Problem domain	Stakeholder's view	State *what* the stakeholders want to achieve through use of the system. Avoid reference to any particular solution.
System requirements	Solution domain	Analyst's view	State abstractly *what* the system will *do* to meet the stakeholder requirements. Avoid reference to any particular design.
Architectural design	Solution domain	Designer's view	State *how* the specific design will meet the system requirements.

for a sailing boat, then early modelling should focus on the vessel and not so much on the radio. This leads to a statement of the problem to be solved in the context of the enclosing solution.

The same principle applies to the systems engineers: they should allow the designers the freedom to perform their role, that of designing against an abstract solution. The elements of solution introduced through functional modelling remain at a high-level, leaving the detail to be defined in subsequent stages.

For example, in a traffic control system:

The stakeholders may express the problem in terms of maximising traffic flow while minimising the risk of accidents at a traffic junction and minimising cost of maintenance.

The systems engineers may consider a variety of solutions, such as bridges, traffic-lights or roundabouts, and a bridge as the approach that best solves the problem within constraints of development and maintenance costs.

The designers then set to work designing the bridge within the physical constraints presented by the physical environment.

It is frequently the case that the stakeholders will express the problem in terms of a preconceived solution. It then becomes the requirements engineers' job to determine whether there is a good reason for mandating a particular solution, or whether it is an unnecessary constraint. For example, the customer starts by trying to procure traffic lights; the supplier asks questions that lead to an understanding of the underlying objectives – maximise traffic flow and minimise risk for drivers and pedestrians – leading to a solution-independent expression of the problem; the reasons for the choice of solution are now better understood, and perhaps confirmed through appropriate modelling, leading to a precise and well-informed specification of the abstract solution.

When it comes to procuring systems, a judgement needs to be made as to whether to procure against the problem domain (stakeholder requirements) or against the abstract solution domain (system requirements). Often the nature of the solution is known in advance, and it makes sense to procure against system requirements framed in terms of that solution. However, even if procuring against a particular solution, the discipline of capturing a statement of the pure problem prior to a solution still offers important advantages.

Without a clear distinction between problem and solution, the following may result:

• Lack of understanding of the real problem
• Inability to scope the system, and understand which functions to include
• Domination of debate about the system by the developers and suppliers, because the only descriptions of the system are expressed in terms of solutions
• Inability to find optimal solutions due to lack of design freedom

For these reasons, the book makes the distinction between stakeholder and system requirements, in terms of how requirements are captured, modelled and expressed.

1.10   How to Read this Book

This book is concerned with engineering requirements and how this process may help those system engineers and software engineers to create better requirements. Chapter 1 has discussed the importance of requirements and has investigated the role of requirements engineering in all parts of the development lifecycle.

Because of multiple dependencies between chapters, the ordering of material has been carefully chosen to reduce the number of forward references. While it is best to read the chapters in the sequence presented, some guidelines are given here to assist readers with particular objectives to make efficient use of the book.

Chapter 2 presents requirements engineering in a generic form that is applicable to all layers of development. While this approach assists the reader in gaining a good understanding of the essence of requirements engineering, it remains, of necessity, quite abstract. The generic process is, however, made more concrete in Chapters 5 and 6, where it is adapted to the stakeholder and system layers of development using numerous examples.

Chapter 3 talks about system modelling, covering various techniques and methods in wide use. This is again in preparation for Chapters 5 and 6, where particular modelling techniques are placed in the context of stakeholder and system requirements.

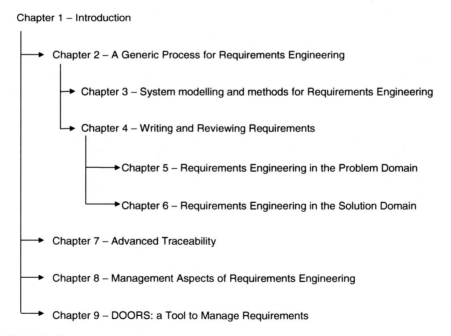

Fig. 1.12 Chapter dependencies

Chapter 4 addresses the structuring of requirements documents, and the expression of requirements statements. Here the language of different kinds of requirement is discussed.

Chapter 5 instantiates the generic process to address the problem domain, in which stakeholder requirements are the primary focus.

Chapter 6 then does the same for requirements in the solution domain, from system requirements downwards through subsystems and components.

Chapter 7 presents further approaches to traceability, aimed at improving the way in which rationale for traceability is captured, and discusses metrics that can be derived from traceability.

Chapter 8 addresses project management in a requirements management context, covering a variety of organisation types.

Finally, Chapter 9 provides an overview of DOORS as an example of a software tool which serves as an enabler of a requirements management process. A case study is used to illustrate the processes presented in the book, and features of the tool.

Figure 1.12 depicts the chapter dependencies.

Chapter 2
A Generic Process for Requirements Engineering

If you can't describe what you are doing as a process,
you don't know what you're doing.

William Edwards Deming,
management consultant, 1900–1993 AD

2.1 Introduction

This chapter introduces the concept of a process for the development of systems. It starts by examining the way in which systems are developed. This leads to the identification of a development pattern that can be used in many different contexts. This development pattern is expressed as a generic process and is explained in some detail. Subsequent chapters indicate how the generic process can be instantiated for specific purposes. The relationship between process models and information models is also explored and an information model for the generic process is developed.

2.2 Developing Systems

Before any system can be developed it is essential to establish the need for the system. If the purpose of a system is not known, it is unclear what sort of system will be developed, and it is impossible to determine whether the system, when developed, will satisfy the needs of its users. Forest Gump summed it up quite nicely when he said:

> If you don't know where you are going, you are unlikely to end up there.

The rigour with which the need is expressed will depend upon the nature of the individual responsible for stating the need and his/her role within the organisation in which they work. The need may be expressed in fairly vague terms initially, e.g. "I would like a system that improves the efficiency of my department". Clearly, such a "specification" is not appropriate to be used as the basis for going out to buy a system. However, it could be the basis for a study to determine exactly what the person

E. Hull et al., *Requirements Engineering*, DOI 10.1007/978-1-84996-405-0_2,
© Springer-Verlag London Limited 2011

really wants. Such a study would have to determine where the department is currently inefficient and to postulate how the capabilities to be provided by the proposed system would be used to improve the efficiency. These activities, which transform a vague statement of need into a set of requirements that can be used as the basis for purchasing a system, constitute the process of developing the Stakeholder Requirements. Stakeholders include people, who will directly interact with the system, but also other people and organisations that have other interests in its existence. The topic of creating Stakeholder requirements is dealt with in detail in Chapter 5.

Figure 2.1 illustrates the development process. In the diagrammatic conventions used for process models, circles (or ovals) represent processes and rectangles represent data or information that is read or produced. The arrows indicate whether data is read or written. Thus, Fig. 2.1 states that the Develop Stakeholder Requirements process takes the Statement of Needs and produces the Stakeholder Requirements. It also creates and reads a Use Model.

Once a sound set of Stakeholder Requirements exist that define what the stakeholders want to be able to do with the proposed system, it is possible to begin to think about potential solutions. Rather than jumping straight to a design, it is good practice to first determine what characteristics the system must have irrespective of the final detailed design. This process is known as establishing the System

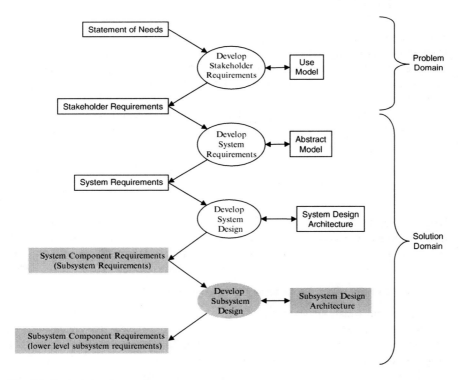

Fig. 2.1 System development process

Requirements. It is recommended that an abstract model of the proposed system be produced. This model provides a basis for discussion within the development team and hence provides a means of establishing a common understanding of the proposed solution, albeit at an abstract level. The model can also be used to explain the solution concepts to those Stakeholders who wish to be assured that the developers are moving along the right lines. Finally, the model provides a structure for presenting the system requirements in a document form. Each element in the model can form a section in the document. This places each requirement in a relevant context and is an indispensable aid to reviewing the complete requirements set from a consistency and completeness point of view.

From the system requirements it is possible to consider alternative design architectures. A design architecture is expressed as a set of interacting components that collectively exhibit the desired properties. These properties are known as the emergent properties of the system and should exactly match the desired characteristics of the system as expressed in the system requirements. The design architecture defines what each system component must do and how the system components interact with each other to produce the overall effects specified in the system requirements. In other words, the design architecture defines the requirements for each system component (see Fig. 2.1) in terms of their functionality and interaction obligations. The design architecture and hence the system component requirements must also stipulate any other required properties such as physical size, performance, reliability, maintainability, etc.

For all but the smallest of systems, the components in the design architecture will be too complex to be implemented directly. Components at this level are frequently known as "subsystems" because they are complex enough to be considered as systems in their own right, but yet they are still only part of the higher-level system for which they are designed.

The process of establishing the design architecture for each subsystem and then using this to derive component requirements is similar to that described for the overall system. Eventually a subsystem design architecture and subsystem component requirements will be produced for each subsystem as indicated in Fig. 2.1.

This description of the development process has indicated that development of systems takes place at several levels and that different activities take place at each level. Figure 2.1 also indicates that each activity is supported by a model (e.g. Use model, Abstract Model, Design Architecture), although the nature of the models differs quite significantly. This is an example of a common aspect: each level of development uses a model. In the following sections of this chapter, these similarities are further explored in order to define the properties of a generic process.

It is essential to realise that there are requirements at each of the levels:

- Needs statement
- Stakeholder requirements
- System requirements
- System component requirements
- Subsystem component requirements

Consequently, requirements engineering is not something that is done once and then forgotten. It happens at each level, and often work is undertaken concurrently at different levels. At all levels from the system components downward, there is multiple concurrent work on requirements at each level. (The grey background of the relevant symbols in Fig. 2.1 indicate this.)

2.3   Generic Process Context

An alternative way of considering the development process is shown in Fig. 2.2. This diagram suggests that the same development process, "Engineer Requirements", is used at each level, although the explanation given above indicates that the work involved is different at each level. This apparently strange way of describing the process is used to introduce the fact that there is, in fact, a significant degree of commonality

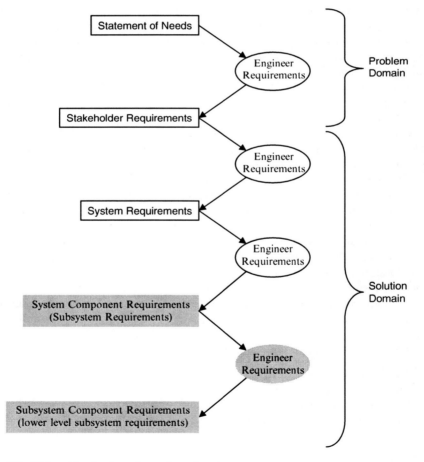

Fig. 2.2 Different levels of requirements engineering

in the work done at each level. The purpose of this chapter is to explore these common aspects and to present a generic process that not only addresses the common aspects but also enables the different aspects to be accommodated.

It is important to stress that in a multi-level development, each level of development demands relevant expertise. At the higher levels, domain knowledge in the problem domain is vital. At the system level, it is important that a system-wide view is taken to avoid too narrow an interpretation of the Stakeholder Requirements. At this level there will inevitably be a solution bias introduced. People or organisations with a proven track record in the development of similar systems are necessary. Similarly, the subsystem developers will bring their own domain experience for the particular specialist area of their subsystem.

Thus, it is unlikely that the same people will undertake development at every level. Even when the same organisation is working on several levels, it is likely that different people will be involved, often from different departments. Therefore, it is useful to introduce the idea that each level of development is done in response to a "customer" at the level above, and will involve "suppliers" at the level below.

2.3.1 Input Requirements and Derived Requirements

Figure 2.3 shows an alternative view of Fig. 2.2 in which the individual processes have been separated. This emphasises that the requirements derived by one process become the Input Requirements of another process and leads naturally to the idea

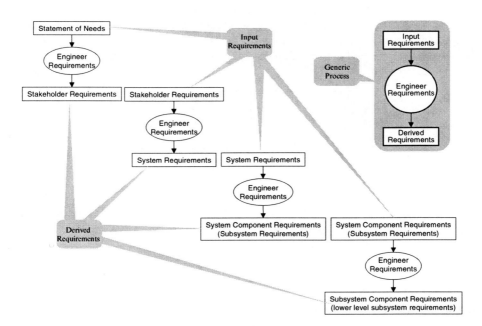

Fig. 2.3 Identifying input and derived requirements of the generic process

that the generic Engineer Requirements process takes in Input Requirements and generates Derived Requirements (also as shown in Fig. 2.3).

2.3.2 Acceptance Criteria and Qualification Strategy

Before moving on to explain the internal details of the Engineer Requirements process, it is necessary to consider another class of information that is both an input to the process and derived by the process. This is information concerning the qualification strategy for the requirements.

To fully understand the significance of requirements and come to a satisfactory agreement that the requirements form a good basis for development, it is necessary to consider how the requirements will be demonstrated when the system (or component) has been implemented. This is partly achieved by determining, for each requirement, the criteria that will be used to establish whether or not the system that claims to implement the requirement is acceptable to the customer.

It is also necessary to determine the circumstances under which the criteria will be examined. In Chapter 1 the notion of test plans at each level was introduced. Testing is just one type of qualification strategy. Others include trials, certification and inspections. The type of qualification strategy to be used will depend on the nature of the system; for example, systems that have safety critical aspects will have to be checked much more carefully than, say, a management information system.

The full context of the Engineer Requirements generic process is therefore as shown in Fig. 2.4.

The Qualification Strategy often introduces new requirements for test equipment, the use of existing facilities (e.g. wind tunnels, anechoic chambers, etc.) and special diagnostic functions or monitor points. In some circumstances a whole new project may evolve to develop the test equipment and other facilities required.

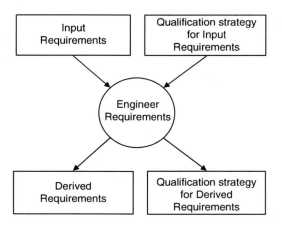

Fig. 2.4 Qualification strategy is essential

For example, in avionics development it is necessary (for cost and safety reasons) to perform as much testing as possible before the equipment is installed in an aircraft. Even when it is installed, it will also be necessary to run with simulations prior to flight trials. Clearly the test pilot must be assured that the avionics will perform to a known standard prior to first flight.

At lower levels in the hierarchy where items are to be manufactured, the qualification strategy may consider issues such as whether the supplier or the customer is responsible for the testing of each item supplied. Possible strategies include full testing of every item prior to delivery, batch testing by the supplier and possible random checks by the customer.

2.4   Generic Process Introduction

Having established the context for the generic process it is now possible to look inside the Engineer Requirements process. The process is introduced firstly in an ideal world in which nothing ever changes and then with modifications to accommodate changes.

2.4.1   Ideal Development

The Engineer Requirements process for the ideal world is shown in Fig. 2.5. The process commences with the need to agree the input information for the project with the customer at the level above. The second activity in the process is to analyse the input information and consider how to develop the outputs required. This activity, which often goes on in parallel with agreeing the requirements, almost always involves the creation of one or more models and leads to analysis reports that together provide a basis for the derivation of requirements and qualification strategy for the lower level supplier(s). These requirements must, when they are sufficiently mature, be agreed with the suppliers to form the basis for a contract for the lower level development.

Figure 2.5 also indicates that there may be several sets of derived requirements generated. Each set must be agreed with the relevant supplier and some suppliers may be responsible for more than one component.

2.4.2   Development in the Context of Change

Unfortunately the world hardly ever stands still. This is especially true in the arena of system development. It seems that everybody is constantly changing his or her mind or finding that what was previously agreed is no longer possible. Therefore

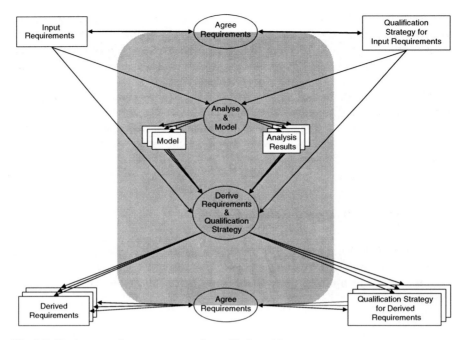

Fig. 2.5 Engineer requirements process for an ideal world

the generic process has to be modified, as indicated in Fig. 2.6, to reflect this necessary evil.

The formality with which change is managed will depend upon the nature and state of the project. During the early stages, changes can and must be made with ease so that progress can be made. However, there comes a time at which a commitment must be made and formal agreement struck. From this time, it is usual to have a more formal arrangement in which changes are not just inserted at the whim of anyone on the project. Instead a process is used in which changes are first requested or proposed and then they are decided upon in the context of their impact on the project. The decision process will usually involve a person such as the project manager, who has the authority to make the decision supported as necessary by a group of people who constitute a change control board. Again the degree of formality with which these people operate will depend on the nature of the project. The topic of change management is addressed in more depth in Chapter 8 in the context of project management.

In Fig. 2.6 it can be seen that almost any activity can lead to the creation of a change and that these changes usually flow upwards. This does not mean that customers never change their minds or that the only problems discovered are lower level detail problems that flow from a top-down strategy. The situation is that the downward path is already accounted for in the normal flows, but the return path has to be explicitly catered for. One typical situation in which a change request might

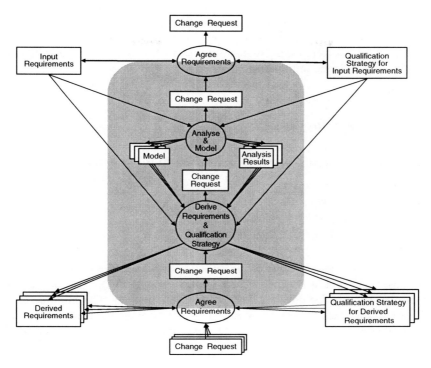

Fig. 2.6 Engineer requirements process in context of changes

arise is, for example, that a limitation in a model or an anomaly in analysis results may well be discovered whilst attempting to generate a derived requirement or the qualification strategy for a derived requirement. A change request will recommend a modification to the model(s) and/or additional analysis work to investigate the problem. Similarly a problem with in input requirement may be identified during the analysis and modelling process leading to the creation of a change request for the Agree Requirements process.

2.5 Generic Process Information Model

Before considering the sub-processes within the generic Engineer Requirements process, it is useful to introduce a generic information model that supports the process.

The diagrams used to represent the generic process contain both process symbols and data or information symbols. The diagrams indicate, via the arrows, which information is being generated and used by each process.

The purpose of an information model is to indicate what types of information exist and whether relationships can or should exist between the items of information.

It is also useful to introduce state transition diagrams to indicate how the state of each type of information can be changed as time proceeds. Consequently these state transition diagrams can give a visual indication of when and how processes interact with each other via the information.

2.5.1 Information Classes

Information types already encountered in the generic process context include:

- Input requirement
- Derived requirement
- Qualification strategy for input requirements
- Qualification strategy for derived requirements
- Change request

Figure 2.7 shows these five types of information expressed as a Unified Modelling Language (UML) class diagram. The name of the class is always shown in the uppermost section (or only section) of the class symbol. The middle section (if present) indicates the names of attributes that the class can have. The bottom section (if present) contains any operations (often called "methods") that can operate on the class.

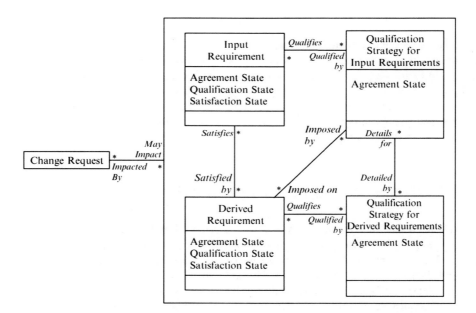

Fig. 2.7 Information model for the generic process

The lines connecting the class symbols show relationships between classes, and these are called Associations in the UML. Thus an Input Requirement can be related to a Derived Requirement by a "Satisfied by" relationship. Similarly the Derived Requirement can be related to an Input Requirement by the inverse "Satisfies" relationship. (These labels are known as "roles" in the UML.) The asterisk indicates that zero or more instances of the class can be involved in the association. Asterisks at both ends indicate that the association can be many to many. Thus in the model of Fig. 2.7 zero or more Input Requirements can be satisfied by a Derived Requirement and an Input Requirement can be satisfied by zero or more Derived Requirements. Some readers may question the zero lower limit, because it suggests that it is not necessary to have any association. However, if the lower limit were set to 1, this would mean that an Input Requirement could not exist unless it was associated with at least one Derived Requirement. Clearly this is an impossible situation. It is essential that Input Requirements can exist prior to Derived Requirements being generated. Consequently this is a reasonable model, because there may be times during a project when there will be no links between input requirements and derived requirements – for example, early in the development before the links have been established. However, a project manager would expect that there were links established as soon as possible. This would then indicate that progress had been made and that all derived requirements were justified by being there to satisfy an input requirement, and conversely that all input requirements had been satisfied.

The Qualification strategy classes can each qualify the appropriate type of requirement and the qualification strategy for the derived requirements can provide more details of an Input Requirement qualification. This can occur, for example, in safety critical systems where it may be necessary to perform lower level detailed inspections that contribute to the satisfaction of the higher level qualification criteria.

As mentioned earlier, it is possible that a qualification strategy may lead to the creation of special test rigs. This would be an example of the *imposed on* relationship between the qualification strategy for an input requirement and one or more derived requirements. Further examples of this relationship occur when, in order to be able to check a component, it is necessary to provide a monitor point. Such monitor points are often essential to be able to check the performance (speed, response, throughput, etc.) of a system under operational conditions.

A Change Request can apply to any of the other four classes. Enclosing the four classes inside an outer rectangle and making the relationship line touch this outer rectangle indicates this.

The middle section of the class symbols is used to define attributes that the class will have. The requirement classes each have the three attributes:

- Agreement state
- Qualification state
- Satisfaction state

These are defined in the following sections by means of state chart diagrams. The agreement state of the qualification classes is assumed to have the values: Agreed or Not Agreed.

2.5.2 Agreement State

The state chart for the Agreement state is shown in Fig. 2.8. In this type of diagram each (rounded) rectangle represents the state of a single requirement at some point in its history. The rectangle labelled *Being Assessed* is known as a 'super-state' because it contains other states within it. The lines connecting one state to another indicate transitions that cause the state to change.

The requirement state starts off in the *Proposed* state. When the customer is content that the requirement is sufficiently well formulated to be sent to the supplier, he sends it. The agreement state then enters the *Being assessed* super-state. During this state, the customer and supplier negotiate until an agreed requirement emerges.

Once in the *Agreed* state, the requirement will stay there until either the Customer or the Supplier creates a Change Request. When this happens the requirement's state re-enters the *Being Assessed* state until a new agreed requirement emerges.

Within the *Being Assessed* state, the customer and supplier take turns to suggest alternative forms of the requirement until an agreement is reached. The agreement state will therefore be in one of the two states shown depending on which party is currently making the assessment.

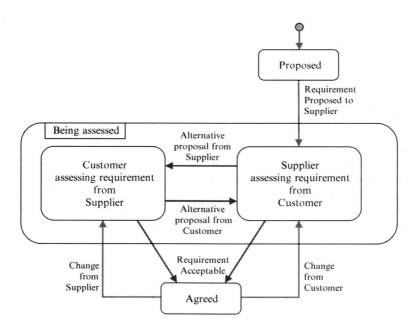

Fig. 2.8 Statechart for agreement state

Fig. 2.9 Qualification state

2.5.3 Qualification State

The qualification state of a requirement is shown in the state chart of Fig. 2.9. The initial state is that there is *No Qualification Strategy decided*. When the qualification strategy has been agreed, the state can proceed to the state *Qualification Strategy decided*. This state can then remain until a change request is received. The change may be directed either at the requirement itself or at the qualification strategy associated with it. When a change is requested, the state becomes *Qualification Strategy suspect* until the impact of the change has been assessed. This assessment determines whether the existing qualification strategy can stand, and the state can return to *Qualification Strategy decided*, or whether an alternative strategy must be decided, in which case the state becomes *No Qualification Strategy decided*.

2.5.4 Satisfaction State

The state chart for the Satisfaction state is shown in Fig. 2.10. The logic of this state is very similar to the qualification states. The starting point is the *Not satisfied* state indicating that no Derived Requirements have been related to this requirement. When the input requirement has been satisfied by one or more Derived Requirements, the lower level supplier agrees the requirement and the higher level (customer) agrees that the Derived Requirements will, indeed, satisfy the Input Requirement, the state can be moved to the *Satisfied* state. It should be noted that there might be many Derived Requirements that have to be agreed before each single Input Requirement can achieve the *Satisfied* state.

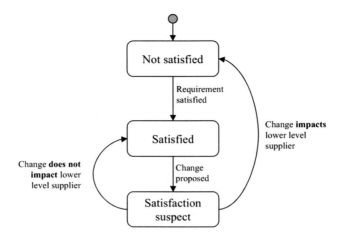

Fig. 2.10 Satisfaction states

When a change is proposed, the Satisfaction state immediately becomes Satisfaction suspect irrespective of whether the proposed change is directed at the higher or lower level requirements. This suspect state is retained until the impact of the proposed change has been assessed and the satisfaction state can then become *Not satisfied* or *Satisfied*.

2.5.5 Information Model Constraints

Change requests bind together the Agreement, Qualification and the Satisfaction state. Registering a change request immediately changes all three states and requires additional work, firstly to determine whether there is any impact, and secondly to address the consequences, if any, of the impact. Note that the Satisfaction state can ripple up and down the requirements that are the subject of the Satisfaction relationship. This ripple effect establishes the potential extent of any consequential change, i.e. the "impact" of the change.

The Agreement state of Derived Requirements must be consistent with the Satisfaction state of Input Requirements, since an Input Requirement cannot achieve its *Satisfied* state until the lower level supplier has agreed all of the Derived Requirements that satisfy it.

2.6 Generic Process Details

2.6.1 Agreement Process

The agreement process is always a concurrent activity between a supplier at one level and the customer at the level above as indicated in Fig. 2.11.

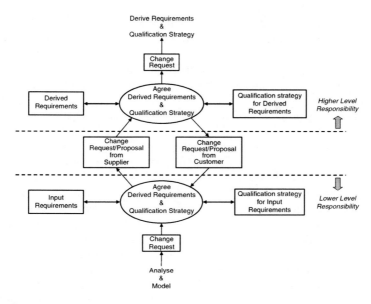

Fig. 2.11 The agreement process

Before any derivation work can commence, it is necessary to assess the Input requirements to ascertain whether they form an adequate basis for the development to proceed.

The assessment must answer the questions:

• Is the requirement complete?
• Is the requirement clear?
• Is the requirement implementable?
• Is the qualification plan clear and acceptable?

Potential answers to these questions lead naturally to the following reasons why a requirement may be rejected:

Missing information – e.g. placeholders such as "TBA" (To be agreed), "TBC" (To be completed) or "TBD" (To be decided) may be used
Lack of clarity – ambiguity, contradiction, confusion, etc.
Impossible to implement – no known solution
Unacceptable qualification plan

Following the review, if a requirement and its qualification plan are acceptable the status can be set to Agreed.

If the requirement is not acceptable then an alternative form is sent to the customer and the onus passes to the customer, and the Agreement state (see Fig. 2.8) becomes "Customer assessing requirement from Supplier". If the customer is content with the alternative wording, then he can set the state to 'Agreed'. If not, then he proposes a further alternative and sends it to the supplier. The Agreement state becomes "Supplier assessing requirement from Supplier", and the onus returns to the supplier.

This process of proposal and counter proposal continues until an agreement is reached. Of course it is possible that agreement may never be reached and a dispute emerges.

When either party proposes a change the "Being assessed" super-state is entered with the onus on the party receiving the change. Negotiation follows as described earlier until a new agreed form can be reached.

During the agreement process, Change Requests may be generated by the customer side to request that the derived requirement is modified. These will pass to the Derive Requirements and Qualification strategy process so that the effect of the change can be assessed and, where necessary, adjustments made to one or more of the derived requirements. Of course it can happen that the change cannot be handled completely at this level and the change may have to be escalated to the Modelling and Analysis process. This need to escalate the decision process up through the levels makes it imperative that people are working at each level. In other words it is necessary to work concurrently on several levels simultaneously. This need completely destroys the notion of the "waterfall" lifecycle in which a sequence of activities takes place in a strict top-down order. Instead of a sequence of activities, development takes place as a concurrent set of negotiations and decision taking.

In many projects the acceptance criteria and qualification plans are only decided quite late. This can be well after the requirements themselves have been agreed and, in some cases, agreement is only reached just prior to the commencement of testing. This is very bad practice and usually leads to delays caused by late changes in requirements to make them testable!

2.6.2   Analyse and Model

Figure 2.12 portrays the Analyse and Model process. The analysis part of this process is primarily concerned with understanding the nature and scope of the input requirements to assess the likely risks involved in satisfying them. Analysis work can range from feasibility studies to explore potential implementation options to the building of prototypes of some vital or high-risk components. It is often necessary to build performance models to investigate potential throughput and response figures.

The other uses of models in this process are to understand the nature of and provide a structure for the derived requirements. The most common models for understanding and structuring Stakeholder Requirements are use cases or User Scenarios. These help to understand how people will use the intended system.

The most common models for structuring solutions in the solution domain are design architectures. These identify elements of the solution and indicate how they interact.

In a lot of cases the model is used to establish the design architecture of the proposed solution. These models are frequently quite obvious for well-established development domains (e.g. automobiles, telecommunications, aircraft, etc.) where a de facto architecture exists. However, for innovative developments where there is no established architecture the model may be more abstract to allow for potential alternatives.

In general, the models used will depend entirely on the nature of the development that is being undertaken. As indicated earlier the types of models used are very much domain specific. In software systems it is increasingly the case that object models are used. Table 2.1 indicates different sorts of models used in three industrial domains.

The point of developing the models is to understand the input requirements together with the proposed qualification strategy and experiment with alternative solution options prior to deciding how to proceed with the creation of derived requirements. This work will also consider possible qualification strategies for the derived requirements and this, in turn, may lead to the creation of requirements for test equipment and/or software. It can also lead to the identification of qualification requirements for the derived requirements.

The Analyse and Model process can be undertaken in parallel with the Agree process since it is likely to generate deeper insight into the nature of the requirements.

In Chapter 3 some widely used modelling techniques are reviewed especially considering those used in the software industry. Chapter 5 explains how to use User Scenario models to aid the understanding of Stakeholder requirements, while Chapter 6 considers function-oriented models that help to provide a framework for system requirements.

During the analysis and modelling process, it is quite likely that further questions will arise concerning the meaning and formulation of input requirements. This gives rise to change requests, which cause the Agree Requirements process to be re-entered.

Table 2.1 Examples of modeling techniques	• Aircraft industry
	  ◦ Aerodynamic model
	  ◦ Three-dimensional spatial model
	  ◦ Weight distribution model
	  ◦ Flight simulator
	• Rail industry
	  ◦ Timetable simulation
	  ◦ Safety, reliability and maintainability models
	• Car industry
	  ◦ Styling model
	  ◦ Dashboard model
	  ◦ Aerodynamic model

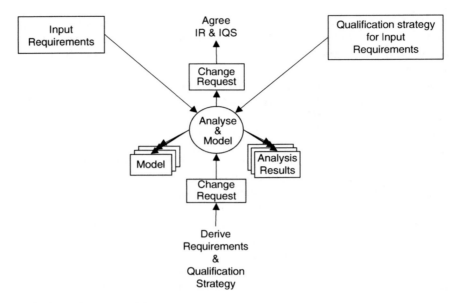

Fig. 2.12 Analyse and model process

2.6.3   Derive Requirements and Qualification Strategy Fig. 2.13 Portrays the Process for Deriving Requirements and Qualification Strategy

2.6.3.1   Deriving Requirements

The way in which the models are used for this purpose varies, but the simplest one to consider initially is the derivation of component requirements based on a design architecture. Here it is possible to determine the specific requirements that must be satisfied by each component. Some of these requirements may be identical to one or more input requirements; others may have been derived from input requirements in order to partition them amongst the components. A further set of requirements consists of constraints imposed either by the component architecture or input requirements. These constraints include interface constraints and possible physical constraints such as mass, volume, power usage and heat dissipation, etc.

In practice, some work on the allocation or derivation of requirements for components may proceed in advance of final agreements on the input requirements and their qualification strategy. However, it is not possible to *complete* this activity prior to final agreement.

In addition to establishing the component requirements, it is also necessary to establish the satisfaction relationship between the input requirements and the derived requirements. This relationship indicates which input requirements are satisfied by which derived requirements and can be used to establish that:

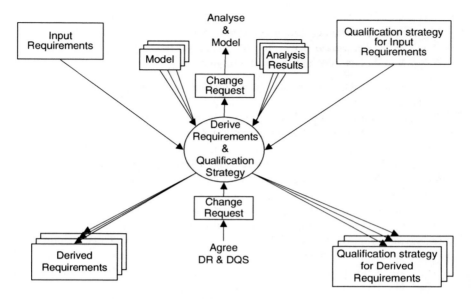

Fig. 2.13 Derive requirements and qualification strategy process

- All input requirements are satisfied.
- All derived requirements are necessary (i.e. they directly or indirectly satisfy one or more input requirements).

It is not sufficient just to assert that a satisfaction link exists, as for example in a cross-reference matrix. The justification for each link should also be stated. These justification statements constitute a satisfaction argument.

During the process of generating requirements from the models, it may become clear that there is a defect or an omission in one or more of the models. This causes a change request to be issued back to the modelling team who will then either modify the model directly or ask for further clarification or change to input requirements. Thus the change escalation process continues.

2.6.3.2 Deriving the Qualification Strategy

As discussed above, the satisfaction relationship is about generating derived requirements from input requirements – how the system is designed. In contrast, the qualification strategy plans how each requirement will be tested at each level.

The qualification strategy consists of a set of qualification actions, each one a particular kind of trial, test or inspection. There may be several qualification actions defined against each requirement.

Each qualification action should take into account the following aspects:

- The **kind** of action that would be appropriate for the requirement.
- The **stage** at which each action could take place, the earlier the better.
- Any special **equipment** that would be needed for the action.
- What would constitute a successful **outcome**?

The qualification plan may be structured either according to the stage or according to the type of action.

The qualification actions defined should be appropriate to the level of requirements. In other words, stakeholder requirements give rise to acceptance trials, whereas system requirements give rise to system tests, i.e. prior to delivery to the customer. It is not necessary to define system tests against stakeholder requirements, since those system requirements derived from the stakeholder requirement will have their own system tests.

Take, for instance, the example shown in Fig. 2.14 in which a system requirement for a ship is decomposed into two requirements on different sub-systems, the hull and the propulsion system. Two qualification tests are planned against the system-level requirement, and two more against the sub-system requirements.

Thus, for a full understanding of how a requirement will be tested, both the satisfaction relationship and the qualification strategy are necessary. To understand the qualification status of a high-level requirement, the results of qualification actions against requirements that flow down from it at all levels have to be taken into account, by making use of the satisfaction as well as the qualification relationship.

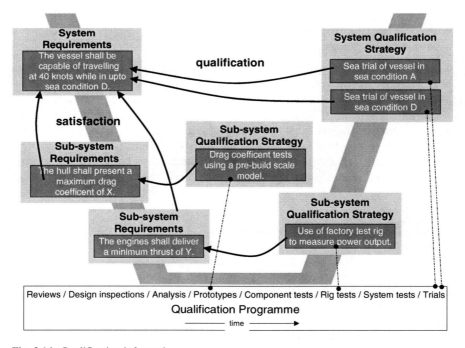

Fig. 2.14 Qualification information

2.7 Summary

A generic process that can be simultaneously applied at each level in a system development has been presented. The benefit of this generic process is that it identifies common actions that are relevant at every level:

- Agreeing input requirements with customer
- Analysis of input requirements to determine the risks and potential pitfalls in satisfying the requirements
- Creating one or more models to investigate possible strategies for deriving requirements
- Generating requirements derived from the input requirements via the analysis and modelling information
- Agreeing the derived requirements with the team(s) that will be responsible for implementing them
- Establishing the satisfaction relationship between Input Requirements and derived requirements
- Establishing the qualification relationship between derived requirements and the relevant qualification strategy

These actions lead to the establishment of information according to the information model presented. The current state of the information can be used to measure progress, to assess the impact of proposed changes and to define metrics on how a project is performing. For example, the state of a requirement can be captured by its three attributes:

- Agreement
- Satisfaction
- Qualification

The ideal state for any requirement in any system development is that it should be:

- Agreed between customer and supplier
- Have a qualification strategy agreed for it
- Be satisfied by lower level requirements (or design)

The extent to which a project's requirements deviate from this ideal state represents the degree of risk to which the project is exposed from the requirements management point of view and also indicates the extent of the work necessary to get the requirements into the ideal state.

Chapter 3
System Modelling for Requirements Engineering

Art and science have their meeting point in method.

Edward Bulwer-Lytton, poet, 1803–1873 AD

3.1 Introduction

System modelling supports the analysis and design process by introducing a degree of formality into the way systems are defined. During system development it is often the case that pictures are used to help visualize some aspects of the development. Modelling provides a way of formalising these representations, through diagrams, by not only defining a standard syntax, but also providing a medium for understanding and communicating the ideas associated with system development.

The art of modelling is arguably the most creative aspect of the work of the systems engineer. There is no 'right' solution and models will evolve through various stages of system development. Models are most often represented visually and the information is therefore represented through connected diagrams. New methods such as object-orientation have advanced the concept of modelling, however most approaches are also based on the principles used and tested over time.

A good model is one which is easily communicated. They need to be used for communication within a development team, and also to an organisation as a whole including the stakeholders. The uses of a model can be diverse and cover a wide spectrum. It might be to model the activities of an entire organisation or to model a specific functional requirement of a system.

Modelling has the following benefits:

- Encourages the use of a *precisely defined vocabulary* consistent across the system.
- Allows system specification and design to be *visualized in diagrams*.
- Allows consideration of *multiple interacting aspects* and views of a system.
- Supports the *analysis of systems* through a defined discipline.
- Allows *validation* of some aspects of the system design through animation.

E. Hull et al., *Requirements Engineering*, DOI 10.1007/978-1-84996-405-0_3,
© Springer-Verlag London Limited 2011

- Allows *progressive refinement* towards detailed design, permitting *test case generation* and *code generation.*
- Encourages *communication between different organizations* by using common standard notations.

Much of the creativity and art of the systems engineer is expressed in the use of modelling techniques. This chapter considers a number of these representations and also some methods for Requirements Engineering that use them.

3.2   Representations for Requirements Engineering

3.2.1   Data Flow Diagrams

Data flow diagrams (DFDs) are the basis of most traditional modelling methods. They are the minimalist graphical representation of the system structure and interfaces and although initially produced for use in data representation and flow, the diagrams can in fact be used to show any type of flow, whether a computer-based system or not. The one output which DFDs do not show is that of control flow.

The elements in a data flow diagram consist of

- Data flows (labelled arrows)
- Data transformations (circles or "bubbles")
- Data stores (horizontal parallel lines)
- External entities (rectangles)

The simple example in Fig. 3.1 shows the use of a data flow diagram in its traditional, information systems context.

Flows represent the information or material exchanged between two transformations. In real-world systems, this may be continuous, on demand, asynchronous etc. When using the notation, diagrams must be supported by textual descriptions of each process, data store and flow.

A *data dictionary* is used to define all the flows and data stores. Each leaf node bubble defines the basic functionality provided by the system components. These are described in terms of a *P-spec* or mini-spec. This is a textual description often written in a pseudo-code form.

The context diagram is the top-level diagram of a DFD and shows the external systems interacting with the proposed system, as in Fig. 3.2.

Bubbles can be decomposed another layer down. Each bubble is exploded into a diagram which itself may contain bubbles and data stores. This is represented in Fig. 3.3.

To illustrate the use of a DFD, consider an example of a context diagram for an Ambulance Command and Control system (Fig. 3.4). This is the starting point for a data-flow analysis of the system.

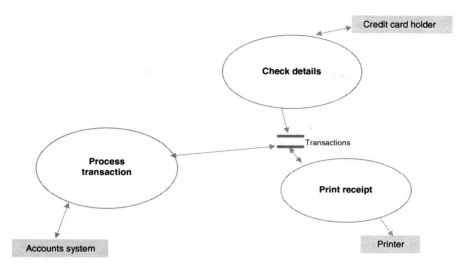

Fig. 3.1 Data flow diagram

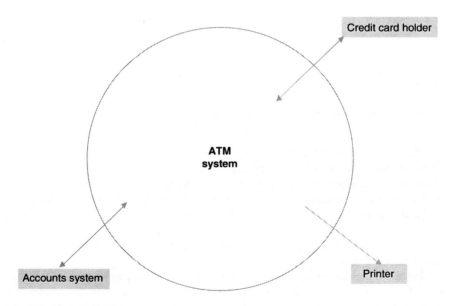

Fig. 3.2 Context diagram

The primary external entities are the *callers*, who make the emergency calls, and the *ambulances*, which will be controlled by the system. Note that *records* are an important output of the system (in fact a legal requirement) and a very important means of measuring "performance".

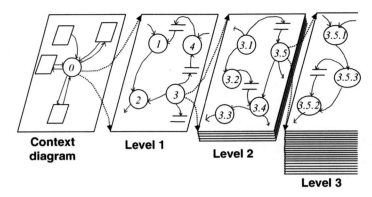

Fig. 3.3 Functional decomposition

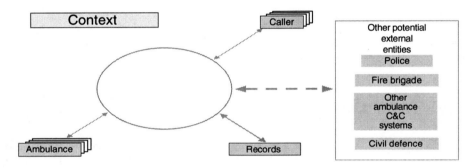

Fig. 3.4 Context diagram for Ambulance C&C System

Other potential external entities that would be required for a real system are shown in the diagram, but for simplicity we shall ignore them.

The next step is to identify the internal functionality of the system. Usually starting by drawing a function for each external entity as the minimal decomposition and then drawing the basic data that must flow between these top-level functions – see Fig. 3.5.

Following this, decomposition of the top-level functions takes place thus including more detail, as shown in Fig. 3.6.

The functional hierarchy in a set of data flow diagrams can be used as a framework for deriving and structuring system requirements. Figure 3.7 shows the functional structure for the Ambulance Command & Control example derived from Fig. 3.6.

Figure 3.7 also indicates some examples of requirements derived from this structure.

The hierarchical breakdown and interfaces give a good view of the component model, but they give a poor view of the "transactions" across the system i.e. from input to output (or to complete some system action) as can be seen in Fig. 3.8.

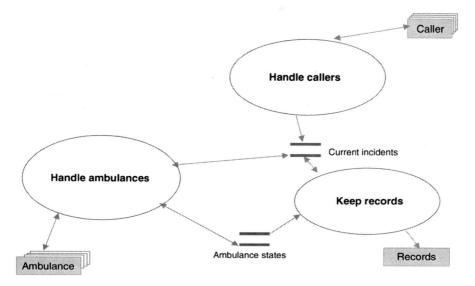

Fig. 3.5 Model for Ambulance C&C system

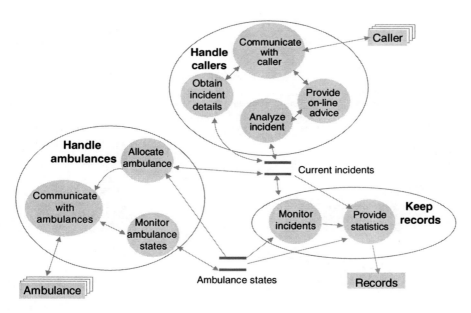

Fig. 3.6 Detailed model for Ambulance C&C system

It is therefore necessary to observe these transactions across the system in terms of the path(s) they follow, the time they take and the resources they absorb. Animating the stakeholder requirements and being able to see which functions are

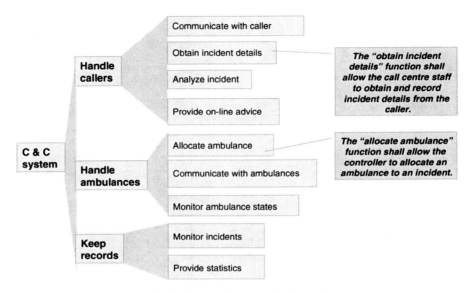

Fig. 3.7 Functional structure for Ambulance Command & Control system

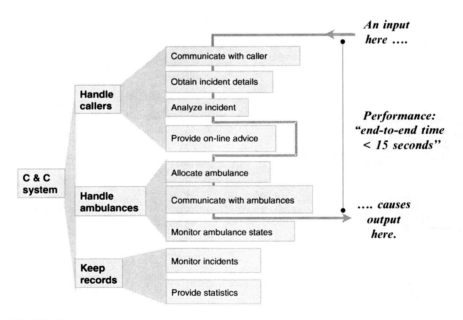

Fig. 3.8 System transactions

operating, will illustrate major transactions, but an alternative way of showing the system transactions is to mark them on to a data flow diagram as shown in Fig. 3.9, using the thick arrows.

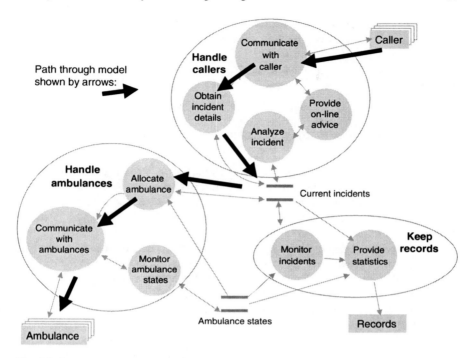

Fig. 3.9 System transactions for Ambulance Command & Control system

DFDs are good at presenting structures but they are not very precise. DFDs are less precise than text for developing a complete definition of a system – interface lines can mean anything, and single words can summarize anything. They cannot handle constraints properly.

A DFD clearly shows functions and interfaces. It can be used to identify end-to-end transactions, but does not directly show them. Ideally we would like to view the diagrams with an "expand in place" approach so that it is possible to view the context in which each level of decomposition is intended to work. Few CASE tools provide this level of facility.

Figure 3.6 actually breaks the conventions for drawing DFDs, because it shows a decomposition of the overall system into several processes and it also shows external agencies with which the system must interact. We advocate a pragmatic use of DFDs, rather than strict adherence to a conceptually pure ideal. To follow precisely the rules for drawing DFDs, the external agencies should appear only in the context diagram, and hence should not be visible at this level. However, the diagram would be far less meaningful if the external agencies were not shown and the flows to them left dangling (which is the defined convention for them).

In summary, DFDs:

• Show overall functional structure and flows.
• Identify functions, flows and data stores.

- Identify interfaces between functions.
- Provide a framework for deriving system requirements.
- Tools are available.
- Widely used in software development.
- Applicable to systems in general.

3.2.2 Entity-Relationship Diagrams

Modelling the retained information in a system, for example flight plans, system knowledge and data base records, is often important. Entity relationship diagrams (ERDs) provide a means of modelling the entities of interest and the relationships that exist between them. Chen (1976) initially developed ERDs. There is now a very wide set of alternative ERD notations.

An *entity* is an object that can be distinctly identified such as: customer, supplier, part, or product. A *property* (or *attribute*) is information that describes the entity. A *relationship* has cardinality, which expresses the nature of the association (one-to-one, one-to-many, many-to-many) between entities. A *subtype* is a subset of another entity, i.e. a type X is a sub-type of Y if every member of X belongs to Y.

ERDs define a partial model of the system by identifying the entities within the system and the relationships between them. It is a model that is independent of the processing which is required to generate or use the information. It is therefore an ideal tool to use for the abstract modelling work required within the system requirements phase. Consider the example Ambulance C&C system in Fig. 3.10.

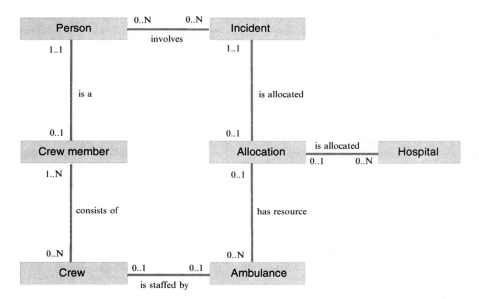

Fig. 3.10 ERD for Ambulance C&C system

3.2.3   Statecharts

Functionality and data flows are not enough for requirements definition. It is also necessary to be able to represent the behaviour of the system and in some circumstances consider the system as having a finite number of possible 'states', with external events acting as triggers that lead to transitions between the states.

To represent these aspects it is necessary to examine what states the system can be in and how it responds to events in these states. One of the most common ways of doing this is to use Harel's Statecharts (Harel 1987).

Statecharts are concerned with providing a behavioural description of a system. They capture hierarchy within a single diagram form and also enable concurrency to be depicted and therefore they can be effective in practical situations where parallelism is prevalent. A labelled box with rounded corners denotes a state. Hierarchy is represented by encapsulation, and directed arcs, labelled with a description of the event, are used to denote a transition between states.

The descriptions of state, event and transition make statecharts suitable for modelling complete systems.

Figure 3.11 presents a statechart for an aircraft flight. The two top-level states are "Airborne" and "On Ground", with defined transitions between them. Inside the "Airborne" state, there are three independent sets of states, while within the

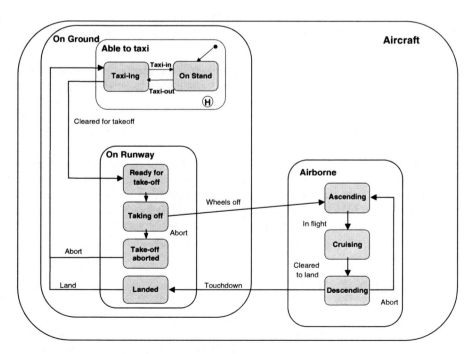

Fig. 3.11 Statechart for aircraft flight

"On Ground" state there are states for "Able to Taxi" and "On Runway". Inside the "On Ground" state, there are further states for 'taxiing' and 'on stand'.

The 'Airborne' state is entered when the aircraft wheels leave the ground and the 'On Ground' state is entered when the wheels touch down. Each of these states can now be further refined in a hierarchical way.

Statecharts introduce one further useful notion, that of history. When a state with the (H) annotation is re-entered, then the sub-state that was exited is also re-entered.

3.2.4 Object-Oriented Approaches

Object-orientation provides a rather different approach from that of the structured analysis approach. *Objects* describe stable (and hopefully) re-usable components.

Object-orientation tries to maximize this re-usability by asking the systems engineer to pick persistent objects i.e. those that can be used in system requirements and design.

So the goals of object-orientation are to:

- Encapsulate behaviour (states and events), information (data) and actions within the same *objects*.
- Try to define *persistent objects*, which can be used within both requirements and design phases.
- Add information by defining the *objects* in more detail.
- Create new objects by specialisation of existing *objects*, not creation of new objects.

Object-orientation focuses on the behaviour of objects, and their inter-relationships. A flat organization of objects is sometimes assumed, but this is not necessary, or even desirable. The analyst looks for entities that are long-lived, and models the behaviour of the system around them. This approach gives a coherent behavioural definition of the system. System elements should be re-usable because the elements (if not their behaviour) can be incrementally enhanced.

Some methodologists insist that design (and even implementation) is refinement of the analysis models. This can be a tall order for non-trivial systems. However, the progression from analysis, design to implementation is often far clearer in object-orientation than in other approaches. More analysis elements end up being represented in the implementation than is common in structured analysis and design. This is a tremendous aid to traceability and maintainability.

3.2.4.1 Class Diagrams

The class diagram is the basic diagramming notation from object-oriented analysis and design. Object-orientation arose out of computer-based simulation. The basic principle is that the contents of a software system should model the real world.

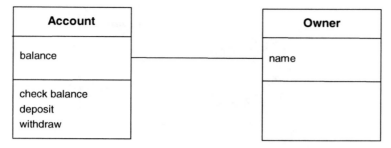

Fig. 3.12 Class diagram

The natural way to handle this is to have *objects* in the software that represent entities in the real world, both in terms of information and actions.

For example, in a banking system, instead of having an accounts file and separate accounts programs, there are *accounts objects* that have information such as *balance* and *overdraft limit* and relationships to other objects such as *account owner*. These objects have *operations* (also called *methods*) to handle the actions that are performed on accounts, like *check balance, deposit, withdraw*, etc.

The original reasoning behind this approach was that it made software development far more akin to modelling, and therefore more natural. As with many good ideas, practicalities intervene, and few object-oriented software systems can be seen as pure representations of the real world. Nevertheless, there is still considerable merit in the method.

A class (or object) diagram is shown in Fig. 3.12.

Class diagrams express information about classes of objects and their relationships. In many ways, they are similar to entity-relationship diagrams. Like them, they show how objects of a certain class relate to other objects of the same or different classes. The principal additional pieces of information are:

- Operations (methods)
- The concept of generalization
- Attributes within the objects

3.2.4.2   Use Cases

Use cases define the interaction that takes place between a user of a system (an actor) and the system itself. They are represented as process bubbles in a DFD type of context diagram. The use case diagram contains the actors and the use cases and shows the relationship between them. Each use case defines functional requirements for the system. Actors do not need to be human, even though they are represented as stick figures, but in fact represent *roles*. Each of the actors will have an association with at least one use case.

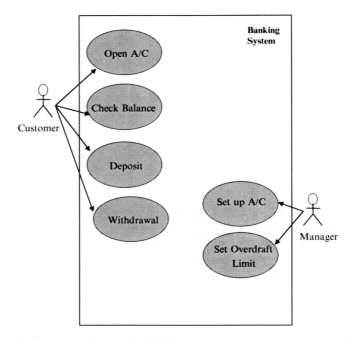

Fig. 3.13 Use case diagram for banking system

The system boundary is also defined on the use case diagram by a rectangle, with the name of the system being given within the box. Normally significant, and useful, textual information is associated with each use case diagram.

Figure 3.13 presents a use case diagram for a banking system.

3.3   Methods

A *method* is a degree more prescriptive than a modelling approach – it tells us what to do to and in what order to do it. Methods use various representations ranging from natural language, through diagrammatic forms to formal mathematics. Methods indicate when and where to use such representations. Those methods that use diagrammatic representations are usually referred to as 'structural methods'; those that use object-orientation are referred to as 'object-oriented methods' and those that use mathematics are referred to as 'formal methods'.

The purpose of the representations used in a method is to capture information. The information capture is aided by defining the set of concepts that a diagram represents, and the syntactic rules that govern the drawing of diagrams.

As we have seen in the earlier sections of this chapter, there are a variety of different representations used for system modelling. Most *methods* – Yourdon (1990), DeMarco (1978), Shlaer and Mellor (1998), Rumbaugh (1991), to name but a few, are a reorganization of these concepts, varying the choice and the order in which they are done, often with minor enhancements. Interestingly, similarities between these methods are far more striking than their differences.

3.3.1 Viewpoint Methods

A viewpoint-based approach to Requirements Engineering recognises that requirements should not be considered from a single perspective. It is built on the premise that requirements should be collected and indeed organised from a number of different *viewpoints*. Basically two different kinds of viewpoint have been proposed:

- Viewpoints associated with stakeholders
- Viewpoints associated with organisational and domain knowledge

The role of the stakeholder is well understood in Requirements Engineering, however viewpoints associated with organisation and domain knowledge may be those associated with some aspect of security, marketing, database system, regulation, standard etc. Such viewpoints are not associated with a particular stakeholder, but will include information from a range of sources.

The following sections consider three different methods based on viewpoints.

3.3.1.1 Controlled Requirements Expression (CORE)

CORE was originally developed following work on requirements analysis carried out for the UK Ministry of Defence. A key finding of this work was that methods often started by defining the context of a solution to a problem, rather than attempting to define the problem itself, before beginning to assess possible solutions. CORE was specifically designed to address the latter approach. Figure 3.14 indicates the concepts and representations used in CORE.

The central concept of CORE is the viewpoint and the associated representation known as the viewpoint hierarchy. A viewpoint can be a person, role or organisation that has a view about an intended system. (This concept has been used as the basis of user viewpoint analysis by Darke and Shanks 1997). When used for system requirements the viewpoints can also represent the intended system, its subsystems and systems that exist within the environment of the system that may influence what the system must do. The viewpoints are organised in a hierarchy to provide a scope and also to guide the analysis process.

If we consider as an example, an aircraft brake and control system (ABCS), then Fig. 3.15 shows a possible list of initial viewpoints arrived at by means of brainstorming.

Having produced a list of potential viewpoints, they are organised into a hierarchy by grouping related candidates. Boundaries are drawn around related sets and this is repeated until all candidates have been enclosed and a hierarchy is produced.

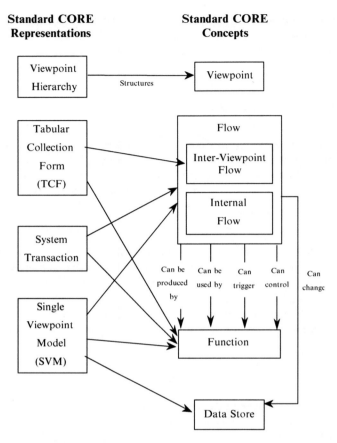

Fig. 3.14 Representations and concepts in CORE

Figure 3.16 shows a partial hierarchy for the aircraft braking control system.

In CORE the actions that each viewpoint must perform are determined. Each action may use or produce information or other items (e.g. commodities) relevant to the system in question. The information generated by the analysis is recorded in a Tabular Collection Form (TCF) as indicated in Table 3.1.

Lines are drawn between adjacent columns to indicate the flows that take place.

Once each viewpoint has been analysed in this way, the TCFs at each level in the viewpoint hierarchy are checked as a group to ensure that the inputs which each viewpoint expects are generated by the source viewpoint and that the outputs which each action generates are expected by the viewpoint(s) indicated as the destination(s) for them.

Returning to the example aircraft braking control system, part of the TCF for the system is shown in Table 3.2.

Further analysis consists of developing a more detailed data flow model for each viewpoint in turn. The starting point for these Single Viewpoint Models (SVMs) is

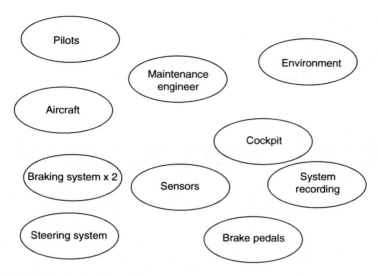

Fig. 3.15 Initial viewpoints for ABCS

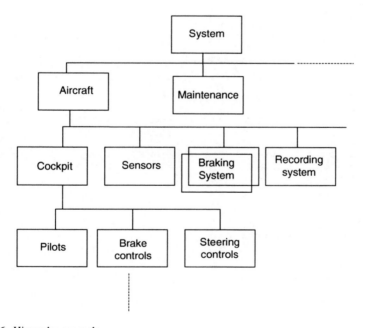

Fig. 3.16 Hierarchy example

the information recorded in the TCFs. SVMs add flows that are entirely within a viewpoint and data stores. The SVMs also define how actions are controlled and triggered by flows from other actions.

Thus the analysis is driven top-down by analysing each stratum in the viewpoint hierarchy. With top-down analysis, it can be difficult to know when to stop and to

Table 3.1 Tabular collection form

Source	Input	Action	Output	Destination
The viewpoint from which the input comes	*The name of the input item*	*The action performed on one or more inputs to generate required outputs*	*The name(s) of any outputs generated by the action*	*The viewpoint to which the output is sent*

Table 3.2 TCF example

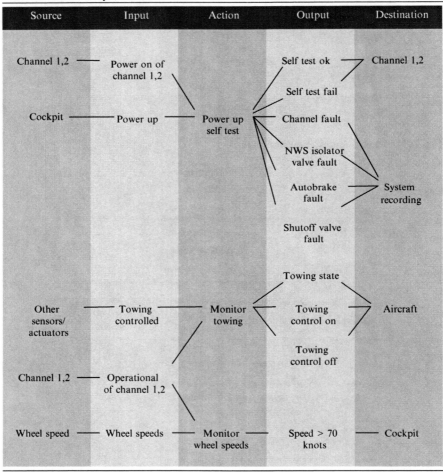

predict where the analysis will lead. The approach of first identifying the viewpoints and then using them to control the subsequent analysis provides a controlled way of doing analysis in a top-down manner. This overcomes a major problem associated with data flow based analysis. This element of control is alluded to in Controlled Requirements Expression, the full name of CORE.

The other main concept of CORE is the *system transaction*. This is a path through the system from one or more inputs, data flows or events to one or more specific output flows or events. The system transactions address how a system is intended to operate. They provide a view orthogonal to the top-down analysis. System transactions provide a sound basis for discussing the non-functional requirements.

3.3.1.2 Structured Analysis and Design Technique (SADT)

SADT is a method of structured analysis, based on the work undertaken by Ross on Structured Analysis (SA) in the 1970s (Ross 1977). It is graphically oriented and adopts a purely hierarchical approach to the problem with a succession of blueprints both modularising and refining it until a solution is achieved. The basic element of SADT is the box, which represents an activity (in activity diagrams) or data (in data diagrams). The boxes are joined by arrows representing either the data needed or provided by the activity represented by the box (in activity diagrams), or the process providing or using the data (in data diagrams).

There are four basic *arrows* associated with a *box*, as shown in Fig. 3.17. The type of arrow is implied by its point of connection to the box:

- *Input* arrows enter the box from the left side, and represent data that is available to the activity represented by the box.
- *Output* arrows exit the box from the right side, and represent data that is produced by the activity represented by the box i.e. the input data has been transformed by the activity represented by the box to produce this output.
- *Control* arrows enter the box from the top, and govern the way in which the transformation takes place.
- *Mechanism* arrows enter the box from below and control the way the activity may use outside mechanisms e.g. a specific algorithm or resources.

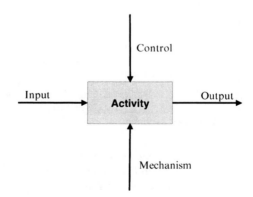

Fig. 3.17 SADT *box* and *arrows*

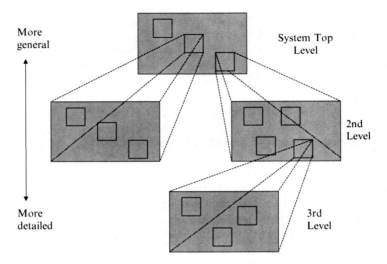

Fig. 3.18 Decomposition using SADT diagrams

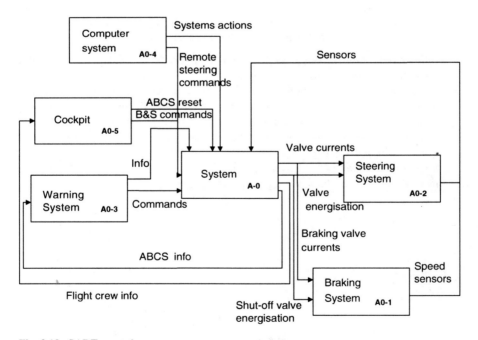

Fig. 3.19 SADT example

An SADT diagram is made up of a number of boxes with the associated set of arrows. A problem is refined by decomposing each box and generating a hierarchical diagram, as shown in Fig. 3.18.

Figure 3.19 shows an example activity diagram for an ABCS. This decomposition proceeds until there is sufficient detail for the design to proceed.

3.3.1.3 Viewpoint-Oriented Requirements Definition (VORD)

VORD (Kotonya 1996) is a method based on viewpoints. The model used is a service-oriented one, where the viewpoints are considered to be clients, if one was to think of it as a client-server system.

A viewpoint in VORD receives services from the system and in turn passes control information to the system. The service-oriented approach makes VORD suited for specifying interactive systems.

There are two types of viewpoint in VORD – **direct** and **indirect**:

- **Direct viewpoints** receive services from the system and send control information and data to the system.
- **Indirect viewpoints** do not interact directly with the system but rather have an 'interest' in some or all of the services delivered by the system.

There can be a large variation of indirect viewpoints. Examples include engineering viewpoints concerned with aspects to be undertaken by the systems engineer; external viewpoints which may be concerned with aspects of the system's environment; organisation viewpoints which may be concerned with aspects of safety etc.

There are three main iterative steps in VORD:

1. Viewpoint identification and structuring
2. Viewpoint documentation
3. Viewpoint requirements analysis and specification

The graphical notation for a viewpoint is shown in Fig. 3.20. A viewpoint is represented by a rectangle, which contains an identifier, label and type. Viewpoint attributes are represented by labels attached to a vertical line dropping down from the left-hand side of the rectangle.

The VORD method guides the systems engineer in identifying viewpoints. It provides a number of abstract viewpoints which act as a starting point for identification. See Fig. 3.21. (Following the convention for VORD diagrams, direct viewpoints are unfilled rectangles and indirect viewpoints are in greyscale). This class hierarchy is then pruned to eliminate viewpoint classes which are not relevant to a particular problem. The system stakeholders, the viewpoints representing other systems and the system operators are then identified. Finally, for each indirect viewpoint that has been identified consideration is given to who might be associated with it.

Based on this approach, Fig. 3.22 gives the viewpoints for a Pay & Display Car Park System.

'Cash User' and 'Credit Card User' viewpoints are specialisations of the 'Car Park Customer' viewpoint. 'Cash Collector' and 'Car Park Manager' are specialisations of

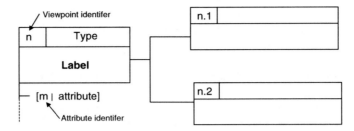

Fig. 3.20 Viewpoint notation

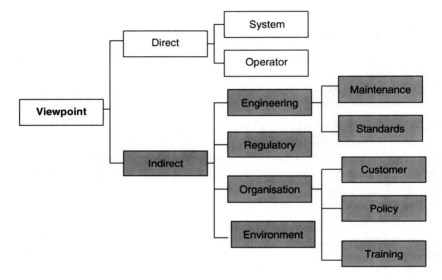

Fig. 3.21 Viewpoint classes

'Car Park Staff'. The 'Ticket Issuing' viewpoint represents the database of the organisation responsible for issuing the pay & display tickets. The 'Credit Card Database' is external and holds details of the customer's credit card details.

The next step in VORD is to document each of the viewpoint requirements. An example of how this is achieved is given in Table 3.3 which shows the initial viewpoint requirements for the 'Car Park Customer' viewpoint. The requirement type refers to a service (sv) or to a non-functional requirement (nf).

VORD also allows for attributes of viewpoints to be provided which characterise the viewpoint in the problem domain. These are important as they provide the data on which the system operates. As stated previously, these are represented on the viewpoint diagram by labels attached to a vertical line dropping down from the left-hand side of the rectangle as shown in Fig. 3.23.

System behaviour is modelled using event scenarios. These describe how the system interacts with the environment and provide a way of describing the complex interactions between the various viewpoints and the system.

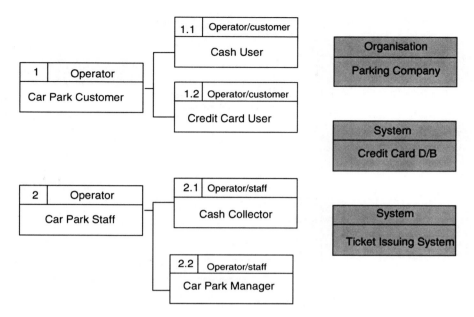

Fig. 3.22 Pay-and-display machine viewpoints

Table 3.3 Requirements from the car park customer viewpoint

Viewpoint			Requirement	
Identifier	Label		Description	Type
1	Customer	1.1	Provide facility for ticket based on suitable payment and length of stay	sv
1.1	Credit card user	**1.1.1**	Provide facility based on valid credit card	sv
		1.1.2	Provide ticket issuing service for customer	sv
		1.1.3	Ticket issuing service should be available 99/100 requests	nf
		1.1.4	Ticket issuing service should have a response time of no more than 30 s	nf
1.2	Cash user			

The final stage of VORD is to translate the results of the requirements analysis process into a requirements document, based on an industry standard.

3.3.2 Object-Oriented Methods

During the late 1980s and early 1990s numerous object-oriented methods emerged proposing different approaches to object-oriented (O-O) analysis and design. The earliest uses of O-O methods were those companies where time to market and

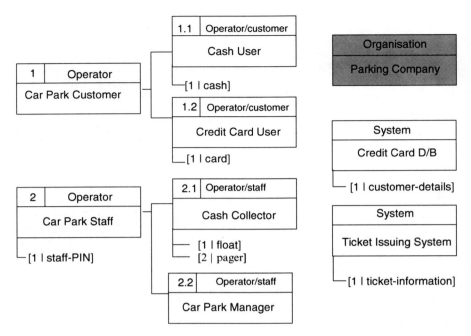

Fig. 3.23 Representation of viewpoint attributes

resistance to change were paramount. They included telecommunications, financial organisations and later aerospace, health care, banking, insurance, transportation etc.

The main players were Object-Oriented Analysis (OOA), Object Modelling Technique (OMT), Booch, and Objectory. Shlaer-Mellor was also there, but would not have been regarded as a truly O-O method. However it did play an important role in assisting in the identification of objects.

3.3.2.1 OOA

Object-oriented analysis (OOA) was developed by Coad and Yourdon (1991a). OOA is spread across three layers, as they are called. The first layer is the subject layer, which is concerned with object identification. Here the users are able to simply represent their understanding of the problem domain by identifying relevant problem domain objects. The second layer, called the attributes layer, is concerned with identifying attributes (data elements) associated with problem domain objects. The third and final layer is the services layer. This specifies the services (or operations) performed by each object.

In effect, OOA helps the systems engineer in identifying the requirements of a system, rather than how the software should be structured or implemented. It therefore describes the existing system, its operation and how the software system should interact with it.

3.3.2.2 OMT

The OMT method was developed by Rumbaugh. It aims to construct a series of object models that refine the system design until the final model is suitable for implementation. The approach is achieved in three phases. The analysis phase produces models of the problem domain. Three types of model are produced – the object model, the dynamic model and the functional model. The object model is the first one to be built. It uses notation similar to that used in OOA, which is based on the concept of ER modelling which describes the objects, their classes and the relationships between the objects. The dynamic model represents the behaviour of the system and uses an extension of Harel's statecharts. The functional model describes how the system functions are performed through the use of DFDs.

These models are arrived at by using an iterative approach. The design phase then structures the model and the implementation phase takes into account the appropriate target language constructs. In this way OMT covers not only the requirements capturing phase but also helps to inform the architectural design process.

3.3.2.3 Booch

The Booch method is one of the earliest O-O methods proposed. Although the method does consider analysis, its strength lies in the contribution it makes to the design of an object-oriented system. The approach is both incremental and iterative and the designer is encouraged to develop the system by looking at both logical and physical views of the system.

The method involves analysing the problem domain to identify the set of classes and objects and their relationships in the system. These are represented using a diagrammatical notation. The notation is extended further when considering the implementation of classes and objects and the services they provide. The use of state transition diagrams and timing diagrams are also an important part of this method.

3.3.2.4 Objectory

Jacobson proposed the Objectory method. Many of its ideas are similar to other O-O methods, but the fundamental aspect of this method is the scenario or *use case*, as described earlier in this chapter. The system's functionality should therefore be able to be described based on the set of use cases for a system – the use case model.

This model is then used to generate a domain object model, which can become an analysis model by classifying the domain objects into three types: interface objects, entity objects and control objects. This analysis model is then converted to a design model, which is expressed in terms of blocks, from which the system is implemented.

3.3.2.5   The UML

The Unified Modelling Language (UML) (OMG 2003) was an attempt to bring together three of the O-O approaches which had gained greatest acceptance – Booch, OMT and Objectory. In the mid-1990s Booch, Rumbaugh and Jacobson joined Rational to produce a single, common and widely usable modelling language. The emphasis was very much on the production of a notation rather than a method or process.

Since its inception the UML has undergone extensive development and change with various versions being launched. UML 1.0 became a standard in 1997 following acceptance by the Object Management Group (OMG). Version 1.3 was released in 1999 and in 2003 the UML 2.0 was released, which is the version used in this book. A discussion of the UML is provided in the following section.

3.3.3   *The UML Notation*

The UML is made up of a number of models, which together describe the system under development. Each model represents distinct phases of development and each will have a separate purpose. Each model is comprised of one or more of the following diagrams, which are classified as follows:

- Structure diagrams
- Behaviour diagrams
- Interaction diagrams

The 13 diagrams of UML2 are shown in Fig. 3.24 and represent all the diagrams which are available to the systems engineer. In reality many will not be used and often only a small subset of the diagrams will be necessary to model a system. Class diagrams, use case diagrams and sequence diagrams are probably the most frequently used. If dynamic modelling is required then activity diagrams and state machine diagrams should be used.

It is how the UML diagrams contribute to modelling which is of interest to us. The purpose of this section is not so much to provide an overview of UML2, but rather to show how models can be used in various aspects of Requirements Engineering.

Consider the banking example used earlier in this chapter. The class is the basic modelling diagram of the UML. Figure 3.25 presents a UML class diagram extending the set of classes to include 'Account', 'Owner', 'Current Account' and 'Issued Cheque' – used to model the system. As shown, each class has an associated set of attributes and operations, i.e. the relationships (in this case, generalisation and association) which exist between one or more classes.

Figure 3.26 gives a different example, that of a Baggage Handling System. This considers the stakeholder requirements which are firmly within the problem domain. When modelling, it is often the case that there are external systems, or

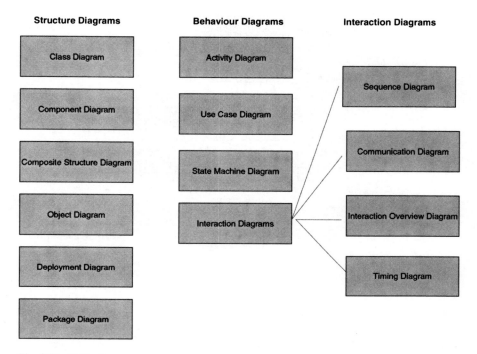

Fig. 3.24 UML diagrams

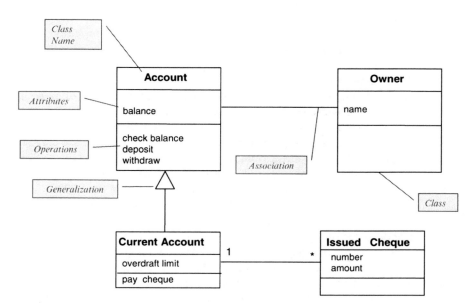

Fig. 3.25 Extended UML class diagram

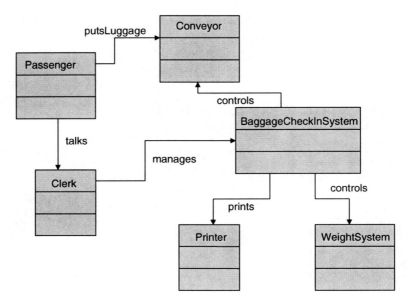

Fig. 3.26 Class diagram for Baggage Handling System

perhaps, devices which the system will use. These can be represented by classes. For the Baggage Handling System, classes are identified such as 'Passenger, 'Clerk', 'Conveyor' etc and also two embedded systems – **BaggageCheckInSystem** and **WeightSystem**. The associations between the systems and other classes serve to define aspects of the system context.

If we turn to the solution domain, then it becomes necessary to reason about function and behaviour. The class diagram therefore needs to be elaborated in order to show these attributes which will be necessary for modelling the system requirements. This is shown in Fig. 3.27.

Use case modelling is used to describe the functional requirements of systems. For our example we will consider two use case diagrams – one for the Baggage Handler System and one for the Baggage Check-in System. Figure 3.28 shows the first of these portrayed as the top-level system. Figure 3.29 is the use case diagram for the Baggage Check-in System. Both diagrams identify their respective system boundaries (marked by a rectangle) and identify the various stakeholders or actors which lie outside the system boundary. It should be noted that the highest level goals of the stakeholders are represented by the use cases. The «include» relationship shows that a use case is included in another use case, indicating the start of hierarchical decomposition.

The UML also provides diagrams to allow the systems engineer to model functionality and behaviour. A sequence diagram shows the interaction and collaboration which exists between objects and thus can model complex behaviour. It is depicted by messages which flow between objects over time. Figure 3.30 shows a sample sequence diagram. The objects are represented by rectangles at the top of

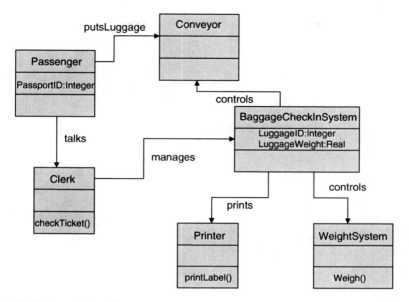

Fig. 3.27 Elaborated class diagram

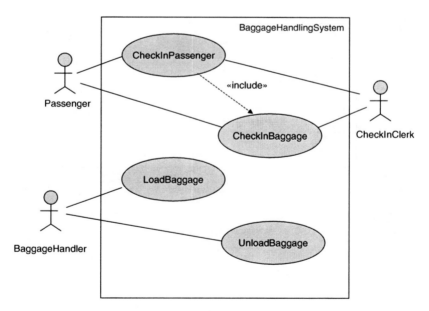

Fig. 3.28 Use case diagram for Baggage Handling System

the diagram and each is attached to a vertical timeline. Messages are ordered by their sequence and are represented by arrows between the timelines. Also included is the feature of an **interaction frame** and the operation 'ref' has been used to

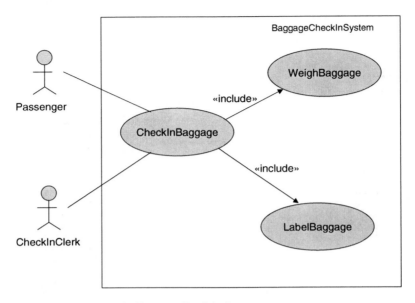

Fig. 3.29 Use case diagram for Baggage Check-in System

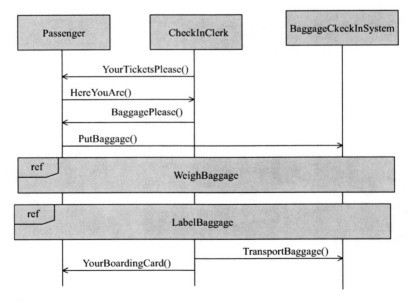

Fig. 3.30 Example sequence diagram

indicate 'reference' i.e. refers to an interaction defined in another diagram, in this case **WeighBaggage** and **LabelBaggage**. These frames have been included to cover the lifelines involved in the interaction.

3.3.4 Formal Methods

Formal methods provide a more rigorous representation based on mathematics, and can be used to conduct mathematical proofs of consistency of specification and correctness of implementation. Rigorous checking is possible, which can eliminate some kinds of errors. This may be necessary in certain types of systems, e.g. nuclear power stations, weapons, and aircraft control systems.

Z (Spivey 1989), VDM (Jones 1986), LOTOS (Bjorner 1987) and the B-Method (Abrial 1996) are the most common formal methods for formal definition of functionality. LOTOS (Language of Temporal Ordering Specification), VDM (the Vienna Definition Language) and Z are formal methods standardized by ISO. B and LOTOS models are executable, and B models can be refined into code.

Formal methods are particularly suitable for critical systems i.e. ones in which potential financial or human loss would be catastrophic, and the cost of applying mathematically rigorous methods can be justified.

Formal methods are slowly becoming more important. If their scope can be broadened to address wider system issues, they will become more useful.

3.3.4.1 Z–A Model-Based Formal Method

Z is a formal specification notation based on first order predicate logic and set theory. The notation allows data to be represented as sets, mappings, tuples, relations, sequences and Cartesian products. There are also functions and operation symbols for manipulating data of these types.

Z specifications are presented in a small, easy to read boxed notation called a 'schema'. Schemas take the form of a signature part and a predicate part. The signature part is a list of variable declarations and the predicate part consists of a single predicate. Naming a schema introduces a syntactic equivalence between the name and the schema. See Fig. 3.31.

Specifications in Z are presented as a collection of schemas where a schema introduces some specification entities and sets out the relationships between them. They provide a framework within which a specification can be developed and presented incrementally.

Figure 3.32 shows a Z specification for the 'issue' operation for a library, where the general behaviour of the overall library system would be specified in a schema

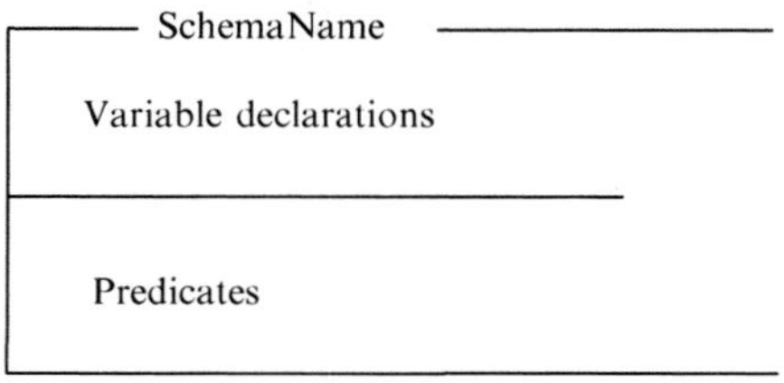

SchemaName

Variable declarations

Predicates

Fig. 3.31 Z schema

Fig. 3.32 Example schema   Library = = [shelved:$\mathbb{P}$ Book:readers:$\mathbb{P}$ Reader:
                                              stock:$\mathbb{P}$ Book: issued:$\mathbb{P}$ Book]

Issue

Δ Library
b? : Book
r? : Reader

---

b? $\in$ shelved; r? $\in$ readers
issued$'$ = issued $\oplus$ {b? - r?}
shelved$'$ = shelved\{b?}
stock$'$ = stock: readers$'$ = readers

---

named 'library'. The notation ΔLibrary is called a delta schema and indicates that the 'Issue' operation causes a state change to occur in the Library.

The schema in Fig. 3.32 distinguishes between inputs and outputs, and before states and after states. These operations are denoted as follows:

'?' denotes the variable as an input to the operation
'!' denotes the variable as an output of the operation

A state after the operation is decorated with the "symbol, e.g. stock" to distinguish it from the state before the operation.

3.4   Summary

This chapter has addressed the issues of system modelling, particularly with respect to the solution domain. A range of techniques and methods have been presented ranging from those which have stood the test of time to those which have been developed more recently. All have been widely used in industry. The contents of the chapter provide a basis for the discussion on modelling stakeholder and system requirements in subsequent chapters.

Chapter 4
Writing and Reviewing Requirements

To write simply is as difficult as to be good.

William Somerset Maugham, author, 1874–1965 AD

4.1 Introduction

Requirements engineering is a technical process. Writing requirements is therefore not like other kinds of writing. It is certainly not like writing a novel, or a book like this; it is not even like the kind of "technical writing" seen in instruction manuals and user guides.

The purpose of this chapter is to present those aspects of writing requirements that are common to every development layer. Wherever the generic process is instantiated, certain principles and techniques are constant in their application to the expression and structuring of requirements.

In writing a requirements document, two aspects have to be carefully balanced:

1. The need to make the requirements document readable
2. The need to make the set of requirements processable

The first of these concerns the structure of the document, how it is organised and how the flow of it helps the reviewer to place individual requirement statements into context. The second focuses on the qualities of individual statements of requirement, the language used to promote clarity and preciseness, and how they are divided into single traceable items.

The experienced requirements engineer comes to realise that a word processor alone is not sufficient to manage a set of requirements, for the individual statements need to be identified, classified and traced. A classic problem, for instance, is the use of paragraph numbers to identify requirements: insert a new one in the middle, and suddenly all the subsequent requirement identifiers have changed.

Equally, those who have tried simply to manage their requirements in a database quickly realise that tables full of individual statements are unmanageable. Despite having the ability to identify, classify and sort requirements, vital contextual information

E. Hull et al., *Requirements Engineering*, DOI 10.1007/978-1-84996-405-0_4,
© Springer-Verlag London Limited 2011

provided by the document has been lost; single statements lose meaning when separated from their place in the whole.

So both aspects – document and individuality – need to be maintained.

The writing and the reviewing of requirements (or any other kind of document, for that matter) should go hand-in-hand, in that the criteria for writing a good requirement are exactly those criteria against which the requirement should be reviewed. Hence the subjects are treated together in this chapter.

4.2   Requirements for Requirements

Before discussing how requirements documents and statements should be written, it is best to review some of the objectives and purpose for the writing of requirements in the first place. This will help in understanding why certain principles are suggested.

The starting place is the identification of stakeholders, which is shown in Table 4.1.

Table 4.1   Stakeholders for requirements

Stakeholder	Role
Author	Creates the requirements and incorporates changes
Publisher	Issues and archives the requirements document
Reviewer	Reviews the requirements and suggests changes
Implementer	Analyses the requirements and negotiates changes

Table 4.2   Abilities required for requirements

Ability
Ability uniquely to identify every statement of requirement.
Ability to classify every statement of requirement in multiple ways, such as:
• By importance
• By type (e.g. functional, performance, constraint, safety)
• By urgency (when it has to be provided)
Ability to track the status of every statement of requirement, in support of multiple processes, such as:
• Review status
• Satisfaction status
• Qualification status
Ability to elaborate a requirement in multiple ways, such as by providing:
• Performance information
• Quantification
• Test criteria
• Rationale
• Comments
Ability to view a statement of requirement in the document context, i.e. alongside its surrounding statements.
Ability to navigate through a requirements document to find requirements according to a particular classification or context.
Ability to trace to any individual statement of requirement.

Table 4.2 lists capabilities required by the various stakeholders that relate to how requirements documents and statements are written. These are the basic things that one needs to be able to do to – and with – requirements, including identification, classification, elaboration, tracking status, tracing, placing in context and retrieving. How requirements are expressed and organised has a great influence on how "useable" the sets of requires becomes.

4.3 Structuring Requirements Documents

Requirements documentation can be very large. On paper, the complete subsystem requirements for an aircraft carrier, for instance, may fill many filing cabinets. It is not unknown for supplier responses to large systems to be delivered in lorries. In such situations, having a well-understood, clearly documented structure for the whole requirements set is essential to the effective management of complexity.

Organising requirements into the right structure can help:

- *Minimize* the number of requirements
- *Understand* large amounts of information
- *Find* sets of requirements relating to particular topics
- *Detect* omissions and duplications
- *Eliminate* conflicts between requirements
- *Manage* iteration (e.g. delayed requirements)
- *Reject* poor requirements.
- *Evaluate* requirements
- *Reuse* requirements across projects

Documents are typically hierarchical, with sections and subsections to multiple levels. Hierarchies are useful structures for classification, and one way of structuring a requirements document is to use the section heading structure to categorise the requirements statements. In such a regime, the position a requirement statement has in the document represents its primary classification. (Secondary classifications can be given through links to other sections, or by using attributes.)

Chapter 3 describes how system models frequently use hierarchies in the analysis of a system. Examples are:

Goal or capability decomposition as in stakeholder scenarios
Functional decomposition as in data-flow diagrams
State decomposition as in state charts

Where requirements are derived from such models, one of the resulting hierarchies can be used as part of the heading structure for the requirements document.

In addition to requirements statements themselves, requirements documents may contain a variety of technical and non-technical text, which support the understanding of the requirements. These may be such things as:

- *Background information* that places the requirements in context
- *External context* describing the enclosing system, often called "domain knowledge"
- *Definition of the scope* of the requirements (what's in and what's out)
- *Definitions of terms* used in the requirement statements
- *Descriptive text* which bridges different sections of the document
- *Stakeholder descriptions*
- *Summary of models* used in deriving the requirements
- *References* to other documents

4.4   Key Requirements

Many organisations use the concept of "key requirements", particularly at the stakeholder level. Often referred to as KURs ("Key User Requirements") or KPIs ("Key Performance Indicators"), these requirements are a small subset abstracted from the whole that capture the essence of the system.

The guiding philosophy when selecting key requirements is similar to that used by Jerome K. Jerome's "Three Men in a Boat", who, when planning for the trip, realised that

> the upper reaches of the Thames would not allow the navigation of a boat sufficiently large to take the things [they] had set down as indispensable. ...
>
> George said, 'We must not think of the things we could do with, but only the things that we cannot do without.'

Every key requirement should solicit a negative response to the question:

> If the solution didn't provide me with this capability, would I still buy it?

or, if at the system level,

> If the system didn't do this, would I still want it?

In this way, the key requirements become those that are absolutely mandatory. (Of course, everything is negotiable, but trading key requirements would always engender very careful consideration.)

Where appropriate, each key requirement should be quantified with performance attributes. Doing this allows them to be used as KPIs, used to assess alternative proposals against the requirements, or used as a summary of vital statistics on project progress.

4.5   Using Attributes

It is clear from the discussions of process in previous chapters, and from the list of abilities in Table 4.2, that a simple textual statement is not sufficient fully to define a requirement; there is other classification and status information that each requirement carries.

Rather than clutter the text of a requirement, additional information should be placed in "attributes" attached to the requirement. Attributes allow the information associated with a single requirement to be structured for ease of processing, filtering, sorting, etc. Attributes can be used to support many of the abilities in Table 4.2, enabling the requirements to be sorted or selected for further action, and enabling the requirements development process itself to be controlled. Figure 4.1 shows an example of a requirement with a number of attributes.

The particular attributes used will depend on the exact processes that need to be supported. Some attributes are entirely automatic – e.g. dates, numbers – some come from users – e.g. priority – other attributes are flags, which are set after analysis work – e.g. checkability.

The following suggestions for attribute categories are drawn in part from some work carried out by a requirements working group in the UK chapter of INCOSE (Table 4.3).

|SH234| The ambulance control system shall be able to handle up to 100 simultaneous emergency calls.

Source:	R. Thomas
Priority:	Mandatory
Release:	1
Review status:	Accepted
Verifiable:	Yes
Verification:	By simulation, then by system test.

Fig. 4.1 Requirements attributes

Table 4.3 Categories of Attributes

Category	Example Values
Identification	
• Identifier	Unique reference
• Name	Unique name summarising the subject of the requirement.
Intrinsic characteristics	
• Basic type	Functional, performance, quality factor, environment, interface, constraint, non-requirement
• Quality factor sub-type	Availability, flexibility, integrity, maintainability, portability, reliability, safety, security, supportability, sustainability, usability, workmanship
• Product/process type	Product, process, data, service
• Quantitative/qualitative type	Quantitative, qualitative
• Life-cycle phase	Pre-concept, concept, development, manufacturing, integration/test, deployment/delivery/installation, operation, support, disposal
Priority and importance	
• Priority (compliance level)	Key, mandatory, optional, desirable *or* Must, Should, Could, Would (MoSCoW)
• Importance	1–10

(continued)

Table 4.3   (continued)

Category	Example Values
Source and ownership	
• Derivation type	Allocation, decomposition
• Source (origin)	Name of document or stakeholder
• Owner	Name of stakeholder
• Approval authority	Name or person
Context	
• Requirements set/document	(Best handled through positioning the requirement in a
• Subject	structured document.)
• Scope	
Verification and validation	
• V&V method	Analysis, inspection, system test, component test
• V&V stage	(See life-cycle phase.)
• V&V status	Pending, pass, failed, inconclusive
• Satisfaction argument	Rationale for choice of decomposition
• Validation argument	Rationale for choice of V&V methods
Process support	
• Agreement status	Proposed, being assessed, agreed
• Qualification status	Not qualified, qualified, suspect
• Satisfaction status	Not satisfied, satisfied, suspect
• Review status	To be reviewed, Accepted, Rejected
Elaboration	
• Rationale	Textual statement about why the requirement is present.
• Comments	Textual comments of clarification.
• Questions	Questions to be posed for clarification.
• Responses	Responses received for clarification.
Miscellaneous	
• Maturity (stability)	Number of changes/time
• Risk level	High, Medium, Low
• Estimated cost	
• Actual cost	
• Product release	Version(s) of product meeting the requirement.

4.6   Ensuring Consistency Across Requirements

A frequent concern in managing large sets of requirements is being able to identify conflicting requirements. The difficulty is in spotting that two statements many pages apart are in conflict. What techniques can be applied to assist in identifying these potential inconsistencies?

One answer lies in classifying requirements in several ways, and using filtering and sorting techniques to draw together small numbers of statements that address the same topic. Many requirements will touch on several aspects of a system. For instance, a requirement primarily about engine performance may also contain a safety element. Such a statement should therefore be viewed in both an engine performance context as well as in a safety context.

To facilitate this, requirements can be given primary and secondary classifications, as discussed in Section 1.3. Typically, each has a single primary classification (perhaps by virtue of its position in the document), and multiple secondary classifications, perhaps using links or attributes.

A thorough review process can now include the systematic filtering of statements by keywords used in primary and secondary classifications. For example, filtering on all requirements to do with safety will draw together statements whose primary classifications may be quite diverse. These can then be reviewed in proximity for potential conflicts.

4.7 Value of a Requirement

Some requirements are non-negotiable. If they are not met, the product is of no use.

Other requirements are negotiable. For instance, if a system is required to support at least 100 simultaneous users, but the delivered solution only supports 99, then it is most likely still of some value to the customer.

Capturing the value of a requirement can be a challenge. A way needs to be found of expressing the idea that, while the target may be 100 simultaneous users, 75 would be acceptable, but anything less than 50 is not acceptable; and maybe 200 would be even better.

One approach to this is to provide several performance values. Here is an example of a three-valued approach:

M: the mandatory lower (or upper) limit
D: the desired value
B: and the best value

These three values can be held in separate attributes, or represented within the text in a labelled form, such as "The system shall support [M:50, D:100, B:200] simultaneous users."

Another approach is to represent the value of a requirement by supplying a function that maps performance to some representation of value, usually a figure between 1 and 100. Figure 4.2 shows four examples of different shapes of value function. Function (a) shows the example above, where the number of simultaneous users should be maximised, but more than a minimum number is mandatory. Function (b) is the binary case: either the performance of 100 is exceeded or not. A performance of 200 does not add extra value. Function (c) shows a performance that is to be minimised (weight, for instance), whereas (d) shows one that is to be optimised (engine revs, for example).

This is a very visual way of presenting value. One glance at the shape of the value curve indicates the nature of the requirement: minimise, maximise, optimise, etc. It also allows the engineers to understand the degrees of freedom they have in designing solutions that deliver the best overall value, by trading-off performance between requirements. This is why this approach is frequently used as part of the tender assessment process, to judge between the relative values of alternative proposals.

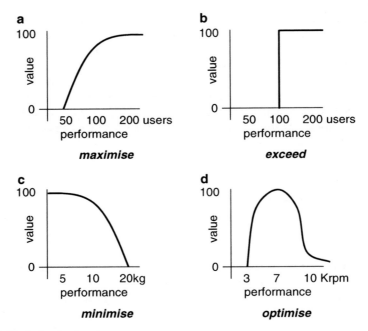

Fig. 4.2 Typical value functions

An attribute can be used to represent a value function as a set of performance/ value pairs.

4.8   The Language of Requirements

The use of consistent language makes it easier to identify different kinds of require- ments. A simple example of this is the use of "shall" as a key word to indicate the presence of a requirement in the text. Some approaches go so far as to use "shall", "should" and "may" to indicate different priorities of requirement.

The language used will vary depending on the level of requirement being expressed. The principle difference is between stakeholder requirements that lie in the problem domain and system requirements that lie in the solution domain (see Chapter 1, Section 1.9).

As is emphasised in Section 1.9, stakeholder requirements are primarily concerned with capability and constraints on capability. A capability statement should express a (single) capability required by one or more identified stakeholder types (or user groups). The types of stakeholder should be stated in the requirement text.

A typical capability requirement takes the following form:

The < stakeholder type > shall be able to < capability >.

Where there are some aspects of performance or constraint associated solely with the requirement, they may also be stated in the text, for instance giving the form:

> **The < stakeholder type > shall be able to < capability >**
> **within < performance > of < event >**
> **while < operational condition >.**

For example, the following capability requirement has a performance and constraint attached:

> **The** *weapons operator* **shall be able to** *fire a missile*
> **within** *3 seconds* **of** *radar sighting* **while** *in severe sea conditions*.

Less commonly, a single performance attribute is associated with several capabilities. For example, several capabilities may need to be provided with a set time. In practice these capabilities are usually sub-divisions of a high-level capability, to which the performance attribute should be attached.

It frequently occurs, however, that constraints have to be expressed separately from the capabilities, either because they apply to the whole system, or because they apply to diverse capabilities. Generally, constraints in stakeholder requirements are based either on minimum acceptable performance or are derived from the need to interact with external systems (including legal and social systems).

A typical constraint requirement takes the following form:

> **The < stakeholder > shall not be placed**
> **in breach of < applicable law >.**

> E.g. **The** *ambulance driver* **shall not be placed**
> **in breach of** *national road regulations*.

Since they lie in the solution domain, the language of systems requirements is a little different. Here the focus is on function and constraints on the system. The language depends on the kinds of constraint or performance associated with the requirement. Here is an example of a function with a capacity performance:

> **The < system > shall < function >**
> **not less than < quantity > < object > while < operational condition >.**

> E.g. **The** *communications system* **shall** *sustain telephone contact*
> **with not less than** *10 callers* **while** *in the absence of external power*.

Here is another that expresses a periodicity constraint:

> **The < system > shall < function > < object >**
> **every < performance > < units >.**

> E.g. **The** *coffee machine* **shall** *produce a hot drink*
> **every** *10 seconds*.

Further discussion of this topic can be found in the following section.

4.9 Requirement Boilerplates

The language of requirements in Section 4.8 was expressed in terms of boilerplates. This section extends this concept, and applies it to the collection and expression of constraint requirements.

Using boilerplates such as the examples in Section 4.8 is a good way of standardising the language used for requirements. A palette of boilerplates can be collected and classified as different ways of expressing certain kinds of requirement. As an organisation gains experience, the palette can be expanded and reused from project to project.

Expressing a requirement through a boilerplate now becomes a process of

- Selecting the most appropriate boilerplate from the palette
- Providing data to complete the placeholders

The requirement can refer to a single document-wide instance of the boilerplate, and placeholders can actually be collected separately as attributes of the requirement. This is illustrated in Fig. 4.3.

From this information, the textual form of the requirement can be generated when needed. Separating the template has the following advantages:

Global changes in style can be effected: To change the ways certain requirements are expressed, only the centrally-held boilerplate needs to be edited.

System information can be processed more easily: Collecting, for instance, all the "<operational condition>" placeholders into a separate attribute allows for easy sorting and filtering on operational conditions.

Confidential information can be protected: In contexts where requirements contain classified or secret information, boilerplates can be used to separate out just those parts of each statement that need to be protected.

This last point merits some elaboration. In military or commercially sensitive projects, there is a need to restrict the availability of some information, but not all. Quite often, a single statement of requirement will contain a mixture of information classified at

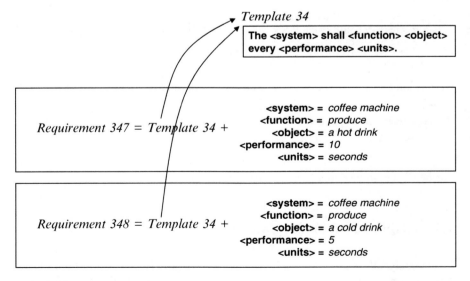

Fig. 4.3 Global templates

various levels. For instance, it is obvious that the ship is going to fire missiles; what is classified is the performance associated with that capability: the state of readiness, the frequency, and the range, etc. Rather than having to hide the whole statement because some of the elements are confidential, boilerplates permit the statement to be visible without some of its more sensitive attributes. Indeed, different readers may be able to see different sets of attributes.

Since there are such a wide variety of constraints, these tend to be the most difficult to express, and this is where boilerplates can help the most. Here is an approach to capturing constraint requirements:

1. Collect all capability requirements first.
2. Construct a list of all the different kinds of constraint that may need to be expressed. If this list is based on past experience of the same kind of system, then boilerplates should exist for each kind. Otherwise suitable boiler-plates may have to be defined.
3. For each capability, consider each kind of constraint, and determine whether a constraint needs to be captured. A large table could be used for this; in each cell, indicate where constraints exist by entering the appropriate sub-ordinate clauses to the requirement; where no constraint is necessary, enter "N/A" in the appropriate cell.
4. Select the boilerplate that best matches the constraint to be expressed, and instantiate it.
5. The process is finished when every "cell" has been considered.

This process answers two frequently asked questions:

- How do I express constraint requirements? (Use boilerplates.)
- How do I know when all constraints have been collected? (Use this systematic coverage approach.)

Table 4.4 shows some examples of boilerplates classified by type of constraint. Note that there may be several ways of expressing similarly classified constraints,

Table 4.4 Example boilerplates for constraint requirements

Type of Constraint	Boiler-Plate
Performance/capability	The <system> shall be able to <function> <object> **not less than <performance> times per <units>.**
Performance/capability	The <system> shall be able to <function> <object> **of type <qualification> within <performance> <units>.**
Performance/capacity	The <system> shall be able to <function> **Not less than <quantity>** <object>
Performance/timeliness	The <system> shall be able to <function> <object> **within <performance> <units> from <event>.**
Performance/periodicity	The <system> shall be able to <function> **not less than <quantity>** <object> **within <performance> <units>.**
Interoperability/capacity	The <system> shall be able to <function> <object> **composed of not less than <performance> <units> with <external entity>.**
Sustainability/periodicity	The <system> shall be able to <function> <object> **for <performance> <units> every <performance> <units>.**
Environmental/operability	The <system> shall be able to <function> <object> **while <operational condition>.**

and that constraints may have a compound classification. Only those parts of the boilerplate that are in bold font are actually relevant to the constraint.

4.10   Granularity of Requirements

The use of requirements boilerplates encourages the practice of placing some constraints and performance statements as sub-clauses of capability or functional requirements. In some cases, it may be desirable to create traceability to and from just those sub-clauses.

This raises the question of granularity of information. How far do we "split the atom" in requirements management?

Statements of requirements can be decomposed into sub-clauses, as long as tool support ensures that clauses are always visible in context. One scheme is to extend the requirements hierarchy to make the sub-clauses children of the main requirement, as shown in Fig. 4.4. Whereas the main requirement is readable (and traceable) on its own, the sub-clauses, albeit separately referenceable for tracing purposes, make sense only in the context of their "parent" statement.

Traceability can now reference a specific sub-clause, but the clause should only ever be cited with the context of its ancestor statements. For instance, the traceable statements that can be cited from Fig. 4.4, with context in italics, are

The communications system shall sustain telephone contact.

- *The communications system shall sustain telephone contact* with not less than 10 callers.
- *The communications system shall sustain telephone contact* while in the absence of external power.

There may be several ways of organising the hierarchy of clauses. Suppose, for instance, that there are multiple capabilities required "in the absence of external power". Then the arrangement may be as in Fig. 4.5.

Now the traceable statements that can be cited are:

- *While in the absence of external power*, the communications system shall sustain telephone contact.
- *While in the absence of external power, the communications system shall sustain telephone contact* with not less than ten callers.
- *While in the absence of external power, the communications system shall sustain radio contact* with not less than 15 ambulance drivers.

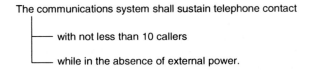

Fig. 4.4 Performance and constraints as sub-clauses

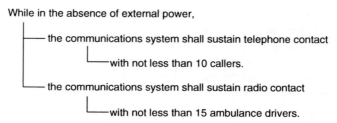

While in the absence of external power,

the communications system shall sustain telephone contact

with not less than 10 callers.

the communications system shall sustain radio contact

with not less than 15 ambulance drivers.

Fig. 4.5 Alternative arrangement of sub-clauses

Indeed, as a general principle, requirements could be organised in such a way that the set of ancestor objects provide the complete context for each statement, including section and sub-section headings.

4.11 Criteria for Writing Requirements Statements

Apart from the language aspects, there are certain criteria that every statement of requirement should meet. These are summarised as follows:

Atomic: each statement carries a single traceable element.
Unique: each statement can be uniquely identified.
Feasible: technically possible within cost and schedule.
Legal: legally possible.
Clear: each statement is clearly understandable.
Precise: each statement is precise and concise.
Verifiable: each statement is verifiable, and it is known how.
Abstract: does not impose a solution of design specific to the layer below.

In addition, there are other criteria that apply to the set of requirements as a whole:

Complete: all requirements are present.
Consistent: no two requirements are in conflict.
Non-redundant: each requirement is expressed once.
Modular: requirements statements that belong together are close to one another.
Structured: there is a clear structure to the requirements document.
Satisfied: the appropriate degree of traceability coverage has been achieved.
Qualified: the appropriate degree of traceability coverage has been achieved.

Two "nightmare" examples of actual requirements are given below.

1. The system shall perform at the maximum rating at all times except that in emergencies it shall be capable of providing up to 125% rating unless the emergency condition continues for more than 15 min in which case the rating shall be reduced to 105% but in the event that only 95% can be achieved then the system shall

activate a reduced rating exception and shall maintain the rating within 10% of the stated values for a minimum of 30 min.

2. The system shall provide general word processing facilities which shall be easy to use by untrained staff and shall run on a thin Ethernet Local Area Network wired into the overhead ducting with integrated interface cards housed in each system together with additional memory if that should be necessary.

Some classic problems are present in these examples. The following pitfalls should be avoided:

- *Avoid rambling*: conciseness is a virtue; it doesn't have to read like a novel
- *Avoid let-out clauses*: such as "if that should be necessary"; they render the requirements useless.
- *Avoid putting more than more requirement in a paragraph*: often indicated by the presence of the word "and".
- *Avoid speculation.*
- *Avoid vague words*: usually, generally, often, normally, typically.
- *Avoid vague terms*: user friendly, versatile, flexible.
- *Avoid wishful thinking*: 100% reliable, please all users, safe, run on all platforms, never fail, handle all unexpected failures, upgradeable to all future situations.

An analysis of the first example above admits that there could be 12 requirements present. A better approach would be to identify clearly the four different operational modes of the aircraft: normal, emergency, emergency more than 15 min, and reduced rating exception, and express a separate requirement for each.

Note the let-out clause in the second example. It is not clear what the scope of the clause is. One interpretation is "The system shall provide general word processing facilities … if that should be necessary." Well is it required, or not?

4.12 Summary

One of the hardest things to do in requirements is to get started. It is important to have an approach, but above all it is important to start writing down the requirements from day 1 and show them to others for comment. The following list is intended as a safe way to proceed:

- Define an outline structure at the outset, preferably hierarchical, and improve it as you go.
- Write down requirements as soon as possible, even if they are imperfect.
- Determine in advance what attributes will be used to classify and elaborate the textual statement.
- Produce an initial version rapidly to stimulate immediate feedback.
- Perfect the requirements as you go, removing repetition, unwarranted design, inconsistency.

- Brainstorm and hold informal reviews continually, with rapid turn-around of versions.
- Exposure to users is much better than analysis by 'experts'.

The rules to follow when writing requirements are as follows:

- Use simple direct language
- Write testable requirements
- Use defined and agreed terminology
- Write *one* requirement at a time

Chapter 5
Requirements Engineering in the Problem Domain

It isn't that they can't see the solution.
It is that they can't see the problem.

Gilbert Keith Chesterton, author, 1874–1936 AD

5.1 What is the Problem Domain?

The problem domain is the domain in which a system is going to be used. Therefore it is important to look at requirements from an operational point of view. A system or any other product enables somebody or some equipment to do something. It is this enabling aspect that is at the heart of requirements engineering in the problem domain. Faced with the challenge of eliciting requirements from potential users one might therefore be tempted to ask a user the question:

What do you want the system to do?

Some users will have little or no idea of what they want the system to do. Those who have an existing system will usually have ideas about how to improve the system, but when there is no existing system this source of inspiration is not available. Answers may be forthcoming from those with insight into what is possible, but they are most likely to come up with a solution because the question is focussing on the functionality to be provided by the intended system.

To avoid this premature jump into the solution domain, it is necessary to ask the question:

What is the purpose of the system you want?

When considering the purpose of a system, people immediately think about what they want to be able to do with the system, rather than how they will do it. What people want to achieve can be stated without any implementation or solution bias and this leaves the solution space open to the systems engineers and architects.

E. Hull et al., *Requirements Engineering*, DOI 10.1007/978-1-84996-405-0_5,
© Springer-Verlag London Limited 2011

It can be argued that even mentioning "the system" in the question could be misleading and the question reduces to:

What do you want to be able to do?

The answers to this question should be of the form:

I want to be able to ...

This is known as a capability requirement and is one of the key forms of requirement in the problem domain.

Having established that requirements engineering in the problem domain is primarily about eliciting capabilities, the next question is

Who should be asked?

This leads to the identification of stakeholders. Recall from the definition in Chapter 1 that a stakeholder is an individual, group of people, organisation or other entity that has a direct or indirect interest (or stake) in the intended system (see Section 1.3.1).

Finally we must examine what sorts of models are relevant to the problem domain. Clearly any models that are used must be understandable to the stakeholders, because they are going to be responsible for validating them. Since the stakeholders have been chosen for their specialist knowledge in the problem, they are generally unwilling or unable to comprehend any model that is the slightest bit technical. For example, if you were to go into a car show room and examine the cars on display, you would be very unlikely to be interested in a state transition diagram of the engine management system. You are more likely to be concerned about the performance of the car in terms of its acceleration, fuel efficiency, its comfort level and the in-car entertainment facilities. In other words, you are considering what the car might be like to drive on a long journey. In your mind's eye you are thinking about an imaginary journey in the car and considering all the aspects of the car that would be useful or beneficial during that journey. This is an example of a use scenario.

It has been found that use scenarios are a very good way of modelling what people do or want to be able to do. They are directly related to the way they think about their job or their problems. The scenario can be constructed with the stakeholders and then used as a basis for discussing the capabilities that are required.

The final aspect of requirements engineering in the problem domain, is that there may be some overriding constraints. In the example of buying a car, you may have a limited budget, or you may require the car to be delivered within a given period of time. You may want the running costs to be below a given level.

It is now possible to consider how to instantiate the generic process for the creation of stakeholder requirements.

5.2 Instantiating the Generic Process

Figure 5.1 contains an instantiation of the generic process for the elicitation of stakeholder requirements. The starting point is the Statement of need. This may be quite a small item, e.g. it could be an email from the Chief Executive Officer (CEO)

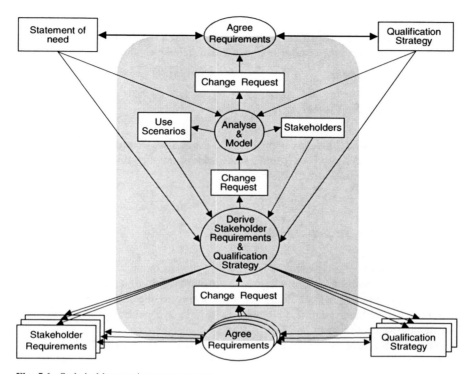

Fig. 5.1 Stakeholder requirements process

to the Chief Technical Officer (CTO) stating that a new product is required to get one step ahead of the competition. Alternatively, there may already have been a study performed to look at possible options and a concept of operations document produced that identifies some use scenarios.

Figure 5.1 indicates that the Analyse and Model process creates a set of Use Scenarios plus a list of the Stakeholders. The derived requirements will be stakeholder requirements.

The details of the *Analyse & Model* and *Derive Stakeholder Requirements and Qualification Strategy* processes are introduced in the following sections.

5.3 Agree Requirements with Customer

The agreement process at the start of the stakeholder requirements process is usually very informal. It is quite likely that the Statement of Needs is a simple document that has not been engineered from a requirements point of view. In other words it is likely to contain woolly expressions of need mixed with descriptive information. It will not contain atomic requirements that can be the target of satisfaction relationships. In this respect the stakeholder requirements process is different to other requirements processes because it starts from this rather vague position. One of the key elements in eliciting stakeholder requirements is to establish the scope of the intended system. This is usually done once a set of use scenarios has been established.

5.4 Analyse & Model

The Analyse & Model process is instantiated for the problem domain as shown in Fig. 5.2. The first activity is to identify stakeholders and then the Use Scenarios can be created in consultation with them.

5.4.1 Identify Stakeholders

As indicated earlier, a stakeholder can be any person or organisation that has an opinion, a responsibility for, or who may be influenced or affected by the proposed system. The types of stakeholders vary according to the nature of the system; e.g. on whether the system is a consumer product, or a public service such as air traffic control or a railway.

People who have an opinion about the proposed system include those people who will use the system directly. Note that this can include the general public who may be passengers on aircraft or trains, or may be affected by a crash when they were otherwise not involved in travelling. People with responsibility for a system may be managers in charge of operating the system, or safety authorities.

The following list contains possible stakeholder categories that can be used as the basis for establishing whether a complete list of stakeholders has been identified.

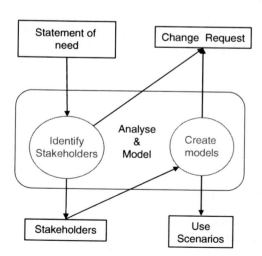

Fig. 5.2 Analyse & Model process for Stakeholder Requirements

The list does not claim to be complete, but provides guidance to help when brainstorming to create the list:

Managers: People who have a responsibility for either the development budget or operating budget of the proposed system. It is also a good plan to involve senior policy makers who will take a view on whether the proposed development conforms to the aims and philosophy of the company or organisation.

Investors: People who either have made or are being invited to make a contribution to the funding of the proposed system, or the organisations responsible for developing or operating the system.

System users: Clearly this is a very important group of stakeholders. They have a direct interest in the capabilities provided by the new system or service. Note that there may also be users who do not interact directly with the system. For example, the users of the Hubble telescope are astronomers. They ask for photographs to be taken in specific directions, and they receive the information when it arrives, but they do not directly control the telescope itself. Users of an existing system are also valuable sources of knowledge of problems with that system. They can give invaluable insight into how they would like to see the system improved.

Maintenance and service staff: Although their prime responsibility is to keep the system running once it has been delivered, they do have important requirements that the system must address in order to help them do their job.

Product disposers: This is an increasingly important role as environmental protection legislation develops. Requirements from this source can have a massive impact on design especially with respect to the materials employed.

Training personnel: Like the maintenance staff, these people have a vested interest in making the system easy to use and consequently easy to train people to use. These people may also require the system to be able to work simultaneously in a mode where live data and training data can be mixed without interfering with the safe operation of the system.

System buyers: For public services and other large systems, the person who buys the system may not be involved directly with its development or operation. They will, though, have an important role to play in scoping the system from the point of view of cost versus perceived benefit. For product-based developments, the buyer may be the actual user, e.g. mobile phone user, car driver etc.

Sales and marketing: These people have a vital role to play in formulating the capabilities for new systems, especially for product-based developments, because, for mass produced consumer products, it is not possible to have access to all potential users.

Usability and efficiency experts: These people have a view on how the system can be optimised to make it efficient in use. These factors include ergonomics, ease of learning and, where relevant, ability to be used reliably under pressure (e.g. in air traffic control).

Operational environment experts: Usually a new system is not created to work in a "green fields" situation; it will have to inter-operate with existing systems.

There may also be other environmental aspects such as emission control where the system must not pollute the environment, and conversely, aspects where the system must be able to tolerate the environment in which it is placed (e.g. in extreme weather conditions, submersed in water etc.)

Government: Rules, regulations and laws determine and influence what a system may or may not do.

Standards bodies: Existing and future standards can affect the goals of a proposed system. These may be international such as the GSM mobile phone standards, national standards or internal company standards.

Public opinion and opinion leaders: Different regions of the world have different attitudes. These factors must be recognised where a product is to be marketed in a wide range of countries.

Regulatory authorities: These organisations may require that certain evidence be collected as part of a certification or authorisation process. Examples include the Rail Regulator in the UK and the Food and Drug Administration (FDA) in the USA.

Having arrived at a list of potential stakeholder types, it is necessary to determine which types are relevant and how each stakeholder type can be accessed. In some cases, e.g. system users, it may be possible to have direct access to them. In other cases, e.g. general public, it is not possible. It is necessary to decide, for those that are accessible, who will be nominated as the stakeholder(s); and for those not accessible, who will take on the "role" of that stakeholder and speak on their behalf. This list then constitutes the output Stakeholders from this process (see Fig. 5.2).

5.4.2   Create Use Scenarios

Most conversations are built around a set of assumptions on which the speakers agree. These assumptions can be interpreted to be a model of their mutual understanding. Attempting to discuss requirements in the absence of any agreed ground rules would be unproductive.

One basic structuring mechanism for discussing capability requirements is the operational or use scenario. This produces a structure that is organised hierarchically by time. Stakeholder requirements use the notion of a scenario as a means of establishing a framework in which meaningful dialogue can take place.

The scenario encourages the stakeholders to think about the job that they are doing and how they would like to do it. In effect, they are rehearsing the way they would like to do their job. Once the scenario is agreed, individual requirements can be generated to define precisely what it is the stakeholders would like to be able to do at each point in the scenario.

Scenarios provide an excellent method for exploring requirements with stakeholders. They are inherently about what the stakeholders want to achieve. A scenario is the *sequence of results* produced (or states achieved) through *time* for the stakeholders. As shown in Fig. 5.3 a use scenario may be represented as

Fig. 5.3 Use scenario as
a hierarchy of goals

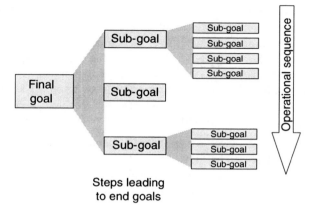

a hierarchy of goals and represents the capabilities provided by the system to the
stakeholders – without saying how to provide them. In other words the use
scenario is a capability hierarchy.

The time-orientation allows a rehearsal of what the system will provide and
the stakeholders can step through and see missing and overlapping elements.
This structure therefore avoids over-commitment to solutions while defining the
problem well.

There is a clearly defined approach to follow when creating use scenarios. The
basic question to ask the stakeholder is "what do you want to achieve?" or "what
state do you want to be in?" The approach is then to start with the final state and
then expand that, by asking what states, or intermediate steps, need to be attained
on the way. The states are then explored as a tree or hierarchy. So the following
procedure emerges:

- Start with the end goal
- Derive the necessary capabilities to get to that point
- Break large steps into smaller steps
- Keep the set hierarchical
- Review informally at each stage
- Be wary of defining solutions

If the stakeholder finds it difficult to define the intermediate stages, the stakeholder
can be asked to describe a typical situation – it is important to know what the stakeholder would do in a situation such as this. If the system is completely new, they
may need to use their imagination. They can postulate what they want or expect to
happen or achieve at each step. It is important at this point also to identify if any
stages are optional, or if there are any repetitions. Would different conditions lead
to different sequences?

The stakeholder also needs to identify the order of the capabilities and whether
this is fixed or variable, and if it is variable, under what circumstances does it vary.
For example, before you can paint a picture you must have paper (or canvas etc.),

paints and brushes, but it does not matter which is ready first. This gives the opportunity to change sequencing or do things in parallel.

It is important, as in all forms of requirements capture, to accept everything that the stakeholders say. It can always be refined later. Frequently it will be necessary to ask the stakeholders to expand on what they mean.

Scenarios represent the capabilities to be provided by the system (in problem domain terms) organised into a hierarchy – without saying how to provide them. They are seen to be beneficial for the following reasons:

Enables stakeholders to step through operational use
Missing steps can be found
Different stakeholders can have different scenarios
Time constructs can be identified

5.4.2.1   Characteristics of Use Scenarios

Figure 5.4 contains an example scenario based on a day out with a sailing boat, which can be transported on a car. It covers all the aspects of the trip starting with loading the boat on to the car, getting ready to sail, sailing and returning home.

The scenario also illustrates some other points:
Generally, it follows a time sequence.

- Its nodes are high level capabilities.
- It shows alternatives.
- It shows periodic repeated behaviour.
- It shows where sequence is not important (parallel branches).
- It shows exceptions.

The use of a time sequence is important. Not only does it provide a simple framework for the stakeholder to understand, but it also helps to place stakeholder requirements into a context.

It is important that all the nodes are expressed as capabilities at the appropriate level. Using the phrase "able to…" in the names of these nodes helps to avoid the tendency to think of the capabilities as functions (and hence to move towards implementation detail).

Scenarios provide a very powerful method of exploring exceptions. In many systems, the functionality to handle exceptions is more complex than that needed to provide the main stakeholder capabilities. The stakeholder can be prompted for exceptions by asking questions such as "what can go wrong in this state?" or "what can go wrong in reaching this state?" Recovery actions can be explored by asking what should be done (or happen) if something does go wrong.

In the example of Fig. 5.4, it can be seen that the scenario includes the need to communicate when the boat is capsized. In the absence of a scenario this requirement may not be spotted.

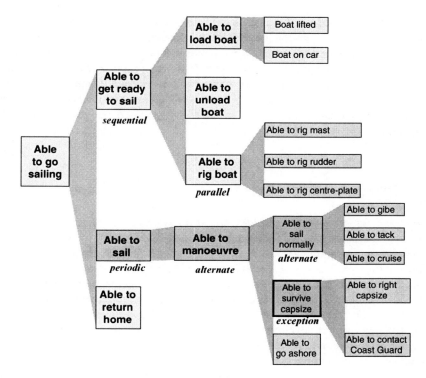

Fig. 5.4 Example use scenario

The example also illustrates how scenarios can make it easy to spot missing areas of requirements. In this case the capabilities of being *able to transport the loaded boat* (to the place where it will be sailed) and being *able to launch* are missing.

The purpose of creating a scenario is to promote understanding and communication. A scenario is not itself a requirement; it is rather a structure for elicitation of requirements. It is an aid to finding a complete set of requirements, by covering every aspect of operational use. Any one modelling technique does not attempt to represent all possible concepts. There is no single correct way of modelling a given operation. Different people come up with different models.

5.4.3 Scoping the System

When preparing the scenarios it is best to set the boundary a bit wider than the anticipated system boundary. This ensures that the view taken is not "blinkered" and serves to set the system in its context. At some point it is essential to determine where the boundary of the system is to be placed and hence to set its scope.

Once the complete set of scenarios has been assembled, the scope of the system can be finalised. This decision may have to be changed, once the cost of developing the system has been estimated. Such estimation can be made by people with experience of system development for the domain of the proposed system. Estimates based purely on scenarios are very coarse and consequently must have a high degree of uncertainty associated with them. Nevertheless making such an estimate can serve to give an initial idea of whether the proposed budget is in the right ballpark.

5.5 Derive Requirements

The *Derive Requirements & Qualification strategy* process has been split into two. These two parts are handled in this section and the next.

The derive Requirements process is instantiated for the problem domain as shown in Fig. 5.5. The key activities are to capture requirements and define a structure into which to place them. Once the structure and the candidate requirements have been decided, it is possible to place the candidate requirements into the structure. In practice the two activities go on in parallel and the structure evolves as experience of using it develops. Therefore, instead of having a separate activity to take the candidates and place them into the structure Fig. 5.5 indicates that both activities contribute to the creation of structured requirements.

When the structure has been completed, the requirements and the structure can be reviewed and refined.

5.5.1 Define Structure

Structure is critical for handling all complex elements in the whole life cycle. Stakeholder requirements are usually captured one by one, cleaned up and then attached into the structure.

Some approaches assume that:

Stakeholder requirements are inherently unstructured.
Traceability to design is enough.
We never see a complete requirements model – requirements need be viewed only one at a time.

These approaches have nothing to do with quality, but are merely in the short-term interests of the developer.

Requirements need to be organised, and there needs to be a good structure to manage the individual requirements as they emerge. The arguments about structure and the need for it are the same for requirements engineering in both the problem

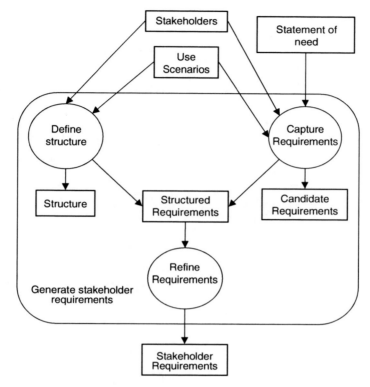

Fig. 5.5 Derive output requirements for problem domain

domain and the solution domain. Therefore they have been put together in Chapter 4. In this chapter it is assumed that providing an understandable structure is vitally important. It remains therefore to indicate how to derive a structure for stakeholder requirements.

The main structuring concept for stakeholder requirements is the use scenario. However, there can be many such scenarios, depending on the nature of the system. It is recommended that time and effort is expended to try and merge scenarios together to make, if possible, a single overall scenario. Obviously this will not always be possible, but it is a good idea to attempt to do it. Apart from any other results, it really makes people aware of the overall extent of the system and frequently exposes many issues.

To explain the way in which scenarios can sometime be merged, an example of running a restaurant will be taken. Three scenarios can be used to describe the restaurant as follows:

• The overall life of the restaurant – Owner's scenario
• A day in the life of the restaurant – Manager's scenario
• A meal at the restaurant – Customer's scenario

Fig. 5.6 Restaurant life
scenario

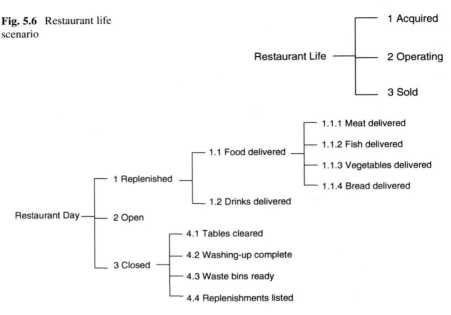

Fig. 5.7 Restaurant day scenario

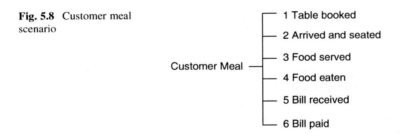

Fig. 5.8 Customer meal
scenario

These are shown in Figs. 5.6, 5.7 and 5.8.

The first goal in the restaurant life scenario is that the owner acquires the restaurant. This is followed by a period of operating the restaurant and finally the restaurant is sold.

The restaurant day scenario considers the states that the restaurant is in during the day. The first goal is to replenish the stocks of food and drink. These aspects of the scenario indicate that there will be several suppliers, but it does not matter which order their deliveries arrive. It could be argued that the completion of replenishment is not necessary before the restaurant is opened, but for the sake of creating a reasonable example it has been decided that no deliveries will be accepted whilst the restaurant is open to customers. The day scenario than has a period of being open and ends the day closed with everything tidied up and the replenishment needs recorded ready for the following day.

The customer meal scenario is a straightforward sequence of states.

If we now examine how these scenarios can be put together, it can be seen that:

- The restaurant day scenario can be a repeating scenario in the Operating state of the restaurant life scenario, and
- The meal scenario can be a parallel repeating scenario in the Open state of the restaurant day scenario.

Thus an overall structure for these three different stakeholder scenarios is shown in Fig. 5.9.

This can then become the structure for the headings of the capabilities in the requirements document.

There are, of course circumstances when it is just not possible to fit scenarios together. There is no easy answer here. If all else fails then all the separate scenarios can be used one after the other. Thus the structure of the Stakeholder requirements document will be a sequence of scenarios, each with their own requirements embedded. Essentially the structure is driven from the list of stakeholders. Even in this approach attempts should be made to nest one scenario inside another.

However, care must be exercised to ensure that there is no duplication. Where there is duplication the duplicated parts must occur once. Two approaches can be used. The first entails cutting out the common items and putting them in a separate section of their own. Then each occurrence must reference the separated section at the appropriate point. The other approach is to place the duplicate section in the first scenario in the document and then reference this from all the other occurrences.

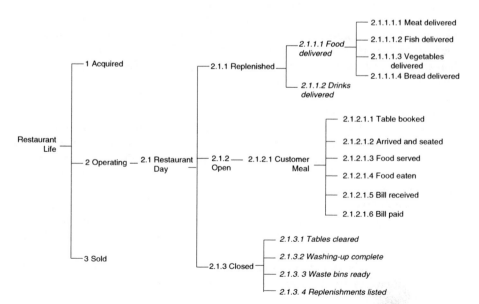

Fig. 5.9 Overall scenario and structure for restaurant capabilities

5.5.2   *Capture Requirements*

5.5.2.1   Sources of Stakeholder Requirements

Stakeholder requirements can come from a variety of sources as illustrated by the following list:

- Interviews with stakeholders
- Scenario exploration (generally through stakeholder interviews)
- Descriptive documentation (perhaps from studies or market research)
- Existing systems which are being upgraded
- Problems and change suggestions from existing systems
- Analogous systems
- Prototyping, either partial systems, mock-ups, or even simple sketches, of the product or the requirements themselves
- Opportunities from new technology (approved by stakeholders)
- Studies
- Questionnaires
- Anthropomorphic studies or analysis of videos

5.5.2.2   Stakeholder Interviews

To undertake this task, the requirements engineer must be a good communicator, able to dig out real requirements from stakeholder interviews. It is an intense psychological task, with little in common with the technical or operational side of system development. It is important to remember that extracting stakeholder requirements is a human, not a technical problem and therefore preparing in advance is important so that the world of the stakeholder is understood.

It is important to talk the stakeholder's language about the stakeholder's world, not about the final product or any technical issues. During the interview the stakeholder should be asked to step through the process of his/her work. A comprehensive set of notes should be taken, which later can be organised into a structured set of requirements and returned to the stakeholder. Interviews are an interactive process, it is important that the requirements engineer should not be judgmental, but should repeatedly ask the question 'Why?' There are several ways of asking this question including: "What is the purpose of this..." or "Can you give me more background on this..." Clearly the requirements engineer is not expected to be an expert in the stakeholder's domain and therefore will need clarification at various points. Don't worry about asking (apparently) stupid questions. The only stupid question is the one that it not asked! It is important, however, that finally the stakeholder will take the responsibility for the requirements.

Discuss scenarios with the people interviewed!

The following provides a set of tips for stakeholder interviews:

- Interview every type of stakeholder.
- Take them seriously.
- Document the interviews and invite stakeholders to sign the record of the interview.
- Identify which scenarios are relevant to the stakeholder(s) being interviewed and talk them through it (them) inviting the interviewee(s) to state what they want to be able to do in each state of the scenario.
- If necessary create new scenarios as the discussion proceeds and then develop requirements from them.
- Attempt to discover the relative importance to the stakeholder of each requirement.
- If the stakeholder is vague about any requirement ask firstly what is the purpose of the requirement and secondly ask how the proposed requirement could be demonstrated.
- Enquire about any constraints the stakeholder is aware of.
- Make stakeholders aware that their requirements will shape the system.
- Stimulate and provoke the stakeholders to respond.
- Don't be judgmental about stakeholder requirements.
- Process the notes into single requirements quickly, and then iterate.

Generally, the questioning will proceed from the general to the specific. It is important to be sure to cover all the ground, defining which areas are irrelevant. Experience in interviewing dictates the form of questioning that takes place, depending on the stakeholder and the situation.

5.5.2.3 Extracting Requirements from Informal Documents

Informal documents such as letters, studies, action lists and other types of descriptive material may all contain requirements hidden in the documentation. Such user requirements should not remain hidden, but should be brought out into the open. But in doing so it is important to record where the stakeholder requirements have come from; in other words the source must be recorded. Further, requirements extracted in this way must be "substantiated" by one of the stakeholders.

5.5.2.4 Identifying Capability Requirements from Scenarios

When an outline scenario has been developed, it is possible to postulate capability requirements directly from them. Sometimes, a simple paraphrase of the state is all that is required. For example, the state *ready to sail* can be paraphrased as the capability *the user shall be able to make the sailing boat ready to sail*. In other cases, more work is required Fig. 5.10 shows some examples, although are not very well formulated. Consider the requirement:

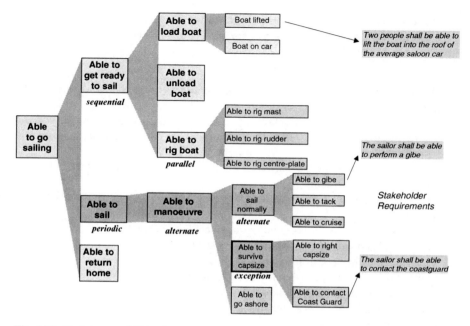

Fig. 5.10 Deriving capabilities from scenarios

Two people shall be able to lift the boat onto the roof of the average saloon car

This raises the questions:

1. How strong are the people?
2. What is an "average saloon car"?

These questions must eventually be answered. However, the important thing when gathering requirements is to write them down. It doesn't matter if there are not well formulated at first – they can always be improved. The critical issue is not to lose the idea! Misquoting a well-known proverb sums up this approach:

A job worth doing is a job worth doing badly!

More information on how to formulate requirements properly can be found in Chapter 4.

5.5.2.5   Requirements Workshops

An alternative way of collecting stakeholder requirements is to hold requirements workshops. This can be an excellent way of rapidly eliciting and capturing requirements. It is important from the outset that the stakeholders are gathered in an environment that is conducive, and that they realise that capturing requirements is not hard and need not take a long time. There should be a structure to the workshop, but

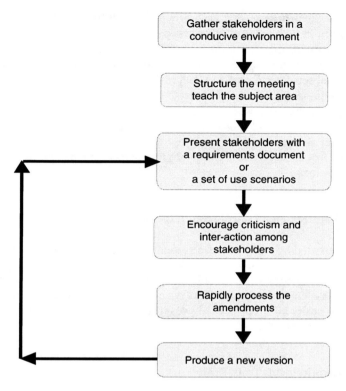

Fig. 5.11 Workshops for requirements capture

it should also be iterative. As shown in Fig. 5.11, stakeholders should be educated to understand what is expected of them. For example, they need to understand the concepts of:

- Stakeholder
- Use scenarios
- Capability requirements

Depending upon the starting point of the workshop, there may be an existing set of requirements already in draft form. Alternatively, start by splitting the attendees into teams and get them to create scenarios for the intended system. Then review the set of scenarios generated with the full group. Make any required changes to the scenarios and then move on to extracting requirements based on them.

As soon as possible present the draft requirements to the full group and encourage criticism and discussion. The possibility of interactions between the different stakeholder groups adds significant value to the requirements. Often this can be the first time that such a group has ever been together. It is always interesting and satisfying when the interactions between the groups leads to the creation of requirements that give a greater insight into what each group wants to be able to do and how these capabilities fit in with those of other groups.

These days with video projectors, the whole group can be involved with editing the requirements online, but it can be more productive to split into smaller groups to work on subsets for a period and then review the whole set together. In this way, for a typical project, a set of requirements can be produced in 3–4 days.

The key element of a workshop is firstly to establish momentum and then to keep it up. Running a workshop can be very demanding, but the results can be very rewarding for all concerned.

It is vital that all stakeholder groups are represented and that they are empowered to make decisions.

5.5.2.6   Requirements Learnt from Experience

Problems reported by real users of a system are gold dust – yet this information is often thrown away. There is somehow a negative attitude to such information because it is associated with a problem, but it can be of real value. Obviously the earlier the problem is detected the less the cost of change, and allowing changes to be made too easily kills a project. However in an iterative development, it is often possible to postpone changes until the next pass through the system.

5.5.2.7   Requirements from Prototypes

Prototypes can be invaluable when creating unprecedented systems. They can be used to give stakeholders an idea of what may be possible. They are also very important in the development of software-based systems where the user interface is difficult to imagine. The problem with prototypes can be that the developers get carried away and spend too much time and effort. Prototype development should therefore always be treated as a small sub-project with its own stakeholder requirements. The objective of the prototype should always be clearly indicated and will usually be to provide greater insight so that stakeholder requirements can be more easily and accurately formulated.

There are three problems with prototyping:

1. The developers get carried away and go into far too much detail.
2. The prototype tends to cause stakeholders to stray into implementation.
3. The stakeholders may be so impressed with the prototype that they want to use it operationally.

The first two problems can be countered by properly formulating the requirements for the prototype. To counter the third problem it is always important to ensure that stakeholders are fully aware of the illusory nature of a prototype, since a prototype can be a partial system, a mock-up, or even a set of simple sketches.

5.5.2.8 Constraints in the Stakeholder Requirements

A constraint is a type of requirement that does not add any capability to a system. Instead it controls the way in which one or more capabilities are to be delivered.

For example, consider the following:

A customer shall be served within 15 minutes of placing the order.

This does not make the system different per se – it just quantifies the service to be provided.

Nevertheless, a word of caution is required here. A mass of constraints, each one reasonable, can make a development impossible, therefore they have to be analysed as a system as well as individually.

When the design is known, each constraint should be analysed for its cost/benefit value or impact upon the system. A constraint may bring a function into existence, for example, a caution and warning system or a backup. The cost of a constraint can only be guessed before the design is known. This unfortunately depends on the design choice, but some minimum assumptions can be made – too many unnecessary constraints can ruin a system.

By default, a constraint applies to the top capability and all its child capabilities inherit it. The applicability should be pushed down the capability hierarchy as much as possible (see Fig. 5.12) to limit its applicability and hence its cost impact. When a constraint applies to just one capability, that constraint can be written as part of the capability.

It is interesting to note the difference between stakeholder constraints and system requirements constraints. Stakeholder constraints refer to the results that the stakeholders want. System constraints are 'professional' or engineering constraints that affect the quality of the product. All of the stakeholder constraints must be addressed in the system requirements. Sometimes they must be reformulated; sometimes they can be passed on without change.

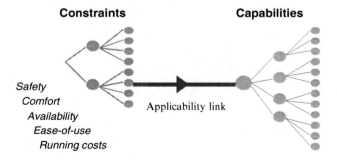

Fig. 5.12 Capabilities and constraints

5.5.2.9 Refine Requirements

Review each requirement in its context and ensure that

1. It belongs in the place it is in.
2. It conforms to the criteria for well-written requirements as explained in Chapter 4.

5.5.2.10 Derive Qualification Strategy

There are two sub-processes used to derive the qualification strategy as shown in Fig. 5.13. These are described in the following subs-sections.

5.5.3 Define Acceptance Criteria

Understanding the criteria that will satisfy the stakeholders that a requirement has been met is an essential and vital part of gathering requirements. Asking the question:

What will convince you that this requirement has been satisfied?

can often lead to a clearer and more focussed formulation of a requirement. This question is therefore often used during stakeholder interviews. The question can be answered in two ways:

1. Stakeholders may define an operational situation in which the requirement can be demonstrated and/or
2. Stakeholders may define a numerical value for a level of achievement that must be demonstrated.

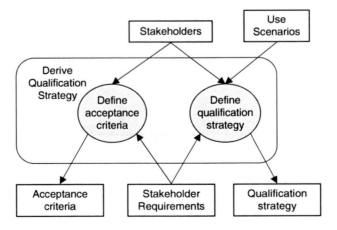

Fig. 5.13 Processes to derive the qualification strategy

The first type of answer feeds directly into the process of creating a set of tests, trials or demonstrations that must be part of the qualification strategy. The second type of answer indicates the "pass mark" for a trial test or demonstration, i.e. it indicates the acceptance criterion for the requirement.

Acceptance criteria define, for each requirement, what would be a successful outcome from the qualification approach adopted. Acceptance criteria are usually recorded in an attribute associated with the requirement. In other words there is usually a one-to-one relationship between a requirement and its acceptance criterion. In the example of the restaurant, the acceptance criterion for the running of the restaurant may be that it is "successful". Success can be measured in a number of ways e.g.:

1. Profitability.
2. Return on investment.
3. Reputation as indicated in guidebooks, newspaper articles, etc.
4. Forward load in terms of how far ahead is the restaurant fully booked.

Different stakeholders may well have differing ideas about success, for example, the owner's bank manager will be more interested in the first two, but the chef will certainly be more interested in the last two.

Thus it is important to determine the acceptance criteria for any requirement from all the stakeholders who may have an opinion.

5.5.4 Define Qualification Strategy

The way in which acceptability is demonstrated depends to a very large extent on the nature of the application and the way in which it has been acquired. For large one-off systems such as air traffic control, it will be necessary to make sure that all the functionality has been properly provided and that the controllers are happy that the system can used easily and quickly when they are busy. This will require a mixture of tests and trials. Firstly the capability of the system under light loading must be demonstrated. If this capability is not acceptable then there is no point in progressing to tests that involve much more investment such as live trials at a busy time of day.

The cost of the qualification strategy must also be borne in mind. Mounting extensive trials is a very costly business and so there must always be a gradual build-up. For example, most ships will undergo harbour trials before sea trials.

The overall cost must also be taken into consideration, but this must be set against the risk of failing to discover a significant flaw in the system during operational use. Thus, where there is a large safety, environmental or financial risk, the qualification strategy must be very carefully engineered to ensure a gradual but steady build-up of confidence in the system. On the other hand, where the consequences of malfunction are quite light, a less expensive approach can be undertaken. The bottom line is that a requirement that cannot be demonstrated (in some way) is not a requirement. Properly engineered requirements are requirements that are easy to understand and demonstrate.

5.6   Summary

Stakeholder requirements must be kept as small as possible and easy to understand. The stakeholder requirements must be non-technical and at the same time realistic. There must be a focus on roles and responsibilities, and it is important to properly distinguish between stakeholder groups.

The common problems that can occur, when deriving stakeholder requirements, are:

- Over-emphasis on solutions.
- Under-emphasis on defining the real problems to be solved.
- Failure to understand that stakeholders must own and approve these requirements.

Stakeholder requirements should be built as quickly as possible, they define the capabilities that the stakeholders require, expressed in terms with which they are comfortable and familiar. There should therefore be a concentration on the stakeholder domain, not on system solutions. They should be structured and traceable to the source of the information. Stakeholder requirements are owned by stakeholders, scoped by the budget holder and often written by requirement engineering specialists.

Chapter 6
Requirements Engineering in the Solution Domain

Never tell people <u>how</u> to do things. Tell them <u>what</u> to do, and they will surprise you with their ingenuity.

George Smith Patton, general, 1885–1945 AD

6.1 What is the Solution Domain

The solution domain is where engineers use their ingenuity to solve problems. The primary characteristic that differentiates the solution domain from the problem domain is that, invariably requirements engineering in the solution domain starts with a given set of requirements. In the problem domain requirements engineering starts with a vague objective or wish list. The extent to which the input requirements for the solution domain are "well formed" depends upon the quality of the people within the customer organisation that developed them. In an ideal world, all the requirements would be clearly articulated, individual test able requirements.

As indicated in Chapter 2, the solution is very rarely arrived it in a single step (see Fig. 6.1).

At each level there is modelling and analysis done to firstly understand the input requirements and secondly to provide a sound basis for deriving the requirements for the next level down. The number of levels of design is dictated by the nature of the application domain and the degree of innovation involved in the development. No matter how many levels are necessary it is always vital to understand how many solution details – the "how" – should be introduced at each step.

At every level in the solution domain, engineers must make decisions that move towards the final solution. Each of these decisions, by their very nature reduces the available design space, i.e. they preclude certain design options, but it is impossible to make progress in the absence of decisions. Engineers are always very strongly tempted to go into too much detail too soon. This temptation must be avoided, in order to allow creativity and ingenuity to work together to produce innovative solutions that could never be achieved in the presence of the constraints imposed by premature design decisions.

E. Hull et al., *Requirements Engineering*, DOI 10.1007/978-1-84996-405-0_6, © Springer-Verlag London Limited 2011

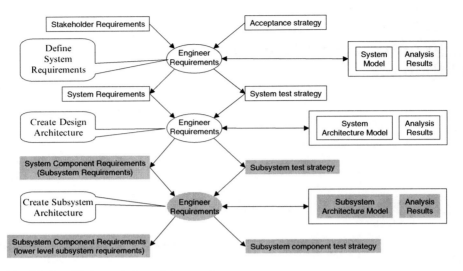

Fig. 6.1 Possible instantiations of the generic process

Typically the first level of system development in the solution domain is to transform the stakeholder requirements into a set of system requirements. These must define what the system must do in order to solve the problems posed by the stakeholder requirements. This first level is illustrated by the top instantiation of the generic process in Fig. 6.1.

The issue of premature design detail is especially problematic at the first step. The System Model indicated in Fig. 6.1 must be created at a level of abstraction that enables the functionality of the system to be defined without going into unnecessary detail.

The next step on from defining the system requirements is to create an architectural design as indicated by the second instantiation of the generic process in Fig. 6.1. This must be expressed in terms of a set of components that interact to generate the emergent properties identified by the system requirements. The derived requirements from the architectural design process (Fig. 6.1) define the requirements that the component suppliers must satisfy for each component.

Development proceeds by further levels of design that move further towards implementation detail.

This chapter concentrates on the transformation from stakeholder requirements to system requirements because it is the most problematic in most developments, because typically too much detail is added too soon.

6.2 Engineering Requirements from Stakeholder Requirements to System Requirements

The full instantiation of the generic model for this transformation is shown in Fig. 6.2.

As with all instantiations, the process commences by agreeing the input requirements, which, in this case, are the stakeholder requirements. The agreement process

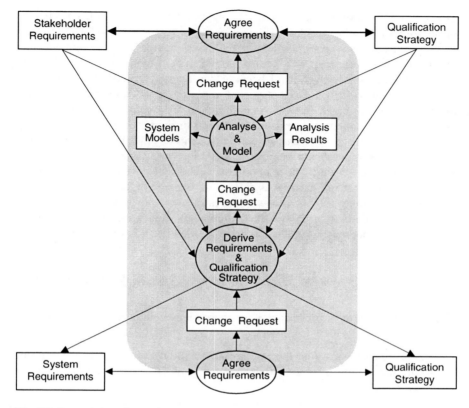

Fig. 6.2 Instantiation of generic process to create system requirements

must not assume that the input requirements have been produced according to the guidelines given earlier in this book. Instead, it is necessary to consider the requirements and the associated qualification strategy on their merits and apply the review criteria for stakeholder requirements with rigour and thoroughness.

6.2.1   Producing the System Model

To avoid the tendency to go into too much detail, engineers should always work in the context of a model (see Fig. 6.1) that is sufficiently detailed for the purpose of defining requirements in terms of what should be done rather than how. The level of detail that should be provided in derived requirements depends upon the level of development at which requirements engineering is being done, but the maxim is always "do not add more detail than is necessary". The temptation to go into detail is always greatest at the top level where Stakeholder requirements expressed in problem domain terms are being translated into high level system requirements that indicate what the system must do to solve the problems posed by the Stakeholders.

The difficulty arises because of the need to work at an abstract level. The creation of an abstract system model, which will provide the framework for the system requirements, always causes problems. At all levels below this, development work progresses in the context of a design architecture. Engineers are much more comfortable with this level of detail, because they can get involved with determining how the system will work. Even at these levels, care must be exercised to ensure that the amount of detail imposed is appropriate. Consequently, the architecture models should be expressed in terms of components that work together, but care should be taken to ensure that components are defined in terms of what they are required to do rather than how they should achieve it. In other words components should be specified as "black boxes" whose internal details are of no concern provided that they achieve their overall purpose as defined in the requirements.

The next sections of this chapter concentrate on the preparation of system models for the derivation of system requirements. Following this, the ways in which the same approach is applied at more detailed levels is explained.

6.2.2   Creating System Models to Derive System Requirements

The system model must be created at an appropriate level of abstraction such that it encompasses:

- Internal functionality that the system must exhibit; this must concentrate on "*what*" the system must do rather than on "*how*" it should be done to avoid pre-empting the design.
- Functionality necessary to enable the system to interact with other systems in its environment.
- Functionality necessary to enable people to successfully interact with it.
- Functionality to prevent the system from malfunctioning due to the presence of other systems (threats) in its environment. (Note that some of these systems may not be deliberately threatening, e.g. electromagnetic emissions from neighbouring equipments.)

This "safeguard" functionality must also prevent the system from interfering in an adverse way with the environment.

The way in which these types of functionality interact with each other and with elements in the system's environment is expressed diagrammatically in Fig. 6.3. It is clear that the context of the system within its environment must be defined with respect to:

- The existing systems with which the new system is required to co-operate
- The types of people who are intended to interact with the system
- The threats that the system must defend against and
- The adverse effects that must be prevented

The functionality can be represented in a number of ways, for example,

- Operations or methods on classes in class diagrams
- Message sequence charts

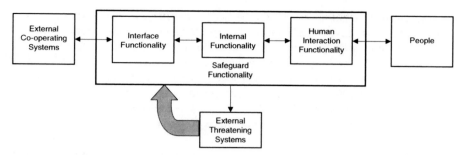

Fig. 6.3 System context and types of functionality

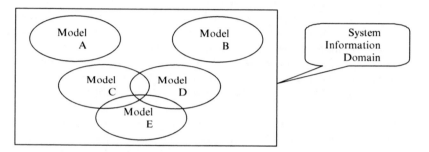

Fig. 6.4 Scope of system models

- State transition diagrams
- Function flow block diagrams
- Processes in data flow diagrams

In practice it will be necessary to use several models in order to cover the many different aspects required. Each model contains information of a defined set of types and each modelling technique carries its own semantics. The information for some models may be quite separate from information in other models. On the other hand the same information may appear in more than one model. In the latter case it is essential that, when information is changed, the change is reflected in all other models in which that information occurs. Ideally this would be achieved automatically by linking the modelling tools. If this is not the case then extreme care should be exercised to ensure that any change is applied *identically* in all relevant models. The Venn diagram in Fig. 6.4 indicates that some models represent islands of information whereas others may have common information presented in different forms. Figure 6.4 also indicates that there may be some system information that is not present in any model.

6.2.2.1 Internal Functionality

This is the primary element of the creation of the system requirements, because it is the main focus of defining what the system will do. It is necessary to create a structure or model that can be the basis for creating the system requirements. This model must have the capability to express some form of decomposition of the system into modules or high-level components such as subsystems. The use of terms such as "module" or "component" tends to make developers think more in terms of implementation rather than specification. This is generally considered to be bad practice, especially in software-based systems. In general systems, the need to move to a more physical model is not considered to be particularly problematic, since the application domain will generally be of a more physical nature.

As an alternative to terminology that may induce premature implementation, there is an increasing tendency (some would say "fashion") to use the term "object" as the decomposition element, especially for software-based systems, since objects can refer to items in the problem domain. This discipline helps to prevent the premature descent into solution terms. Functionality can then be introduced as methods or operations on objects and as interactions between objects.

The use of this object-oriented approach can also make the creation of traceability from the system requirements to the stakeholder requirements an easier task, because the same objects tend to be visible in both the problem domain and the solution domain.

In addition to stating what the system must do, the system model may also be required to indicate the intended behaviour of the system. There are a number of ways in which to represent this type of information. Models in this area usually represent the fact there are a number of concurrently active "actors" that interact in some way. Examples of this sort of notation are message sequence charts and behaviour diagrams. Message sequence charts have long been used in the telecommunications industry. Behaviour diagrams originated in the US ballistic missile early warning system (BMEWS) in the 1970s and have been implemented in tools such as RDD-100 from Ascent Logic Corporation and CORE from Vitech Corporation.

Behaviour can also be modelled using state transition diagrams or state charts. State transition diagrams have the limitation that they can only model a sequence of states and the item being modelled can only be in one of these states at any one time. State transition diagrams cannot represent hierarchical states directly. Separate diagrams must be used for each level in the hierarchy and, in some cases this means that there may be a set of active diagrams at certain times. Such sets of diagrams can be difficult to understand. To avoid this complexity it is better to use state charts because they have been developed to directly handle state hierarchies. They also address parallel states.

In any system it is necessary to consider whether there is information to be handled. Some systems, e.g. insurance company systems, require that information must be gathered and retained for use over a number of years. In other systems, e.g. radar data processing systems for air traffic control, there is some information that has a long lifetime, e.g. flight plans, whereas the current position of an aircraft in flight, by its very nature, soon gets out of date. Thus the information requirements must be examined to ascertain:

- The longevity of the information – i.e. for how long is the information relevant, and for how long must it be retained?
- The freshness of the information – i.e. how up to date must it be (seconds, minutes or hours)?

It is also very relevant to know the amount of information that may be involved. This can have a profound effect on the design of the system.

6.2.2.2 Interface Functionality

It is necessary to define the nature of the interactions required with any other system. Interactions may involve the movement of information, or material between the systems. The movement may be in one direction or both, and there may be limits on the capability that can be transferred. It may be necessary to provide temporary storage (e.g. data buffer or warehouse) for items that are held up. There may be time response requirements on the speed with which either system must react to a stimulus from the other.

The nature of interfaces varies significantly. However, there must always be a baseline reference that indicates what each party undertakes to do or provide as part of the interface. These obligations are frequently documented in an Interface Control Document (ICD). Where the interactions are controlled by national or international standards, the standard becomes the interface control document to which all relevant parties can work. Where the interface is less well defined, the obligations (i.e. interface requirements) must still be written down and agreed. Control of these requirements is notoriously difficult because there is often no organisation with a clear mandate to control the interface. Consequently each party to the interface tends to have its own version of the document and, worse, each party tends to have its own interpretation of it.

It is usual for interface documents to be controlled by the organisation that has responsibility for the system that encompasses the two (or more) systems that interact. Such an organisation is quite difficult to define when a new system is being developed. Often the existing system(s) will have been developed earlier and the interfaces may not be properly documented. Further, the development organisation may well no longer have any responsibility for that system, having handed it over to a higher-level customer or other operating authority.

Care must be exercised to ensure that all interface obligations are accurately reflected in derived requirements at the appropriate level and, so far as is possible, the interface control authority is clearly defined.

6.2.2.3 Human Interaction Functionality

The crucial issue for human interactions with a system is to know what interactions are going to be required. The context in which the users will work is also important.

This can have an impact on the way they can work. For example, users working in a standard office environment will be warm and able to work conveniently without gloves. Other users may have to operate the system in harsh environments such as extreme cold weather, or hazardous situations where protective clothing will be necessary. In these circumstances the design of the displays and keyboards must take note of these aspects.

6.2.2.4   Safeguard Functionality

The environment in which a system must operate will also have a significant influence especially with respect to safety and security. For example, in a banking system it is necessary to provide assurance that information and money will not be given to unauthorised people. In a car (system) it is necessary to be assured that the car will stop when the brake pedal is operated.

There may also be other systems operating in the environment of the system that may be competing with the system being developed. This competition could be commercial competition as in online banking for example. Here the need for any system to be evolved rapidly can be of prime importance.

Other 'competing' systems include those that could interfere with the correct operation of a system by, for example, making radio transmissions that confuse the system or overload sensitive receivers. An example of this is the worry that the use of mobile telephones on board aircraft in flight could interfere with the aircraft's navigation systems.

6.2.2.5   System Transactions

It is worthwhile re-visiting the use scenarios that were developed for the system from the stakeholders, or if none exist to create a set of relevant scenarios. These can be applied to the system model(s) to make sure that they are possible within the system being specified (see Fig. 6.5). Working through these 'system transactions' provides reassurance that elements of system functionality have not been lost by a blinkered approach to object modelling or functional decomposition. (Note that this use of the term "system transaction" is different to the use of the term within the CORE method described in Chapter 3.)

The system transactions shown in Fig. 6.5 as User System Transactions are those derived from the use scenarios. Figure 6.5 also indicates that there can be other transaction derived from the way in which the system being developed must interact with external systems.

System transactions encourage system engineers to stand back and take a 'holistic' view of the system. It is all too easy to concentrate on the detail and forget the big picture i.e. how do the detailed parts work together to achieve the overall aim?

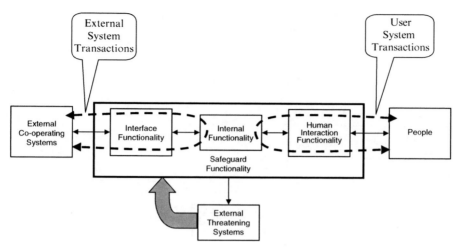

Fig. 6.5 System transactions

6.2.2.6 Modes of Operation

Different functionality may be required in some circumstances. A typical example for information-based systems is the need to be able to provide training for staff without compromising the integrity of the data held in the system. Other examples include fallback modes of operation following a failure or, in military systems, different modes depending on the current state of alertness. These may be related to the use scenarios in the stakeholder requirements.

6.2.2.7 Additional Constraints

In addition to the constraints already mentioned, there are additional aspects that should be considered. Perhaps the most important are those concerned with safety and certifiability. In these areas additional requirements can be introduced and these will certainly have a strong influence on the means adopted for qualification. The relevant authorities will have to be convinced that a system is safe to use or to be deployed, or, in the case of an aircraft, that it can be given a certificate of airworthiness.

A further set of additional constraints are introduced by the need to manufacture the system. It may be necessary to use an existing facility or the design may have to be changed in order to reduce the cost of manufacturing.

6.2.3 Banking Example

In this example of a management information system, the primary concern will be to model the information that must be handled, but it is quite clear that there are many other areas that should be addressed. Several system models are therefore

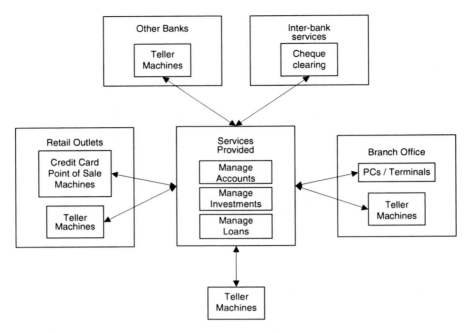

Fig. 6.6 An abstract model for the bank example

likely to be used, one focussing on the information, others focussing on the flow and security of information.

Figure 6.6 shows a model that provides an alternative abstraction for the bank example. It identifies the types of locations where equipment might be sited and thus from where transactions may be initiated.

6.2.3.1 Internal Functionality

The primary internal functionality is concerned with supporting the services provided by the bank such as current accounts, deposit accounts, loans and investment portfolios. To support these services the system must be able to collect, update and retain information. Of vital importance here are the types (or classes) of information (e.g. accounts, customers, etc.), the relationships that exist between them (e.g. how many accounts is a customer allowed to have?) and the longevity, freshness and volume of each type.

It is important to determine how information is collected, disseminated and manipulated.

A further important aspect of a banking system is the number and location of sources of information and/or transactions. These will include branches, automatic teller machines and credit card point of sale machines.

From a performance point of view it is important to understand the likely loading that the system must be able to cope with, such as the number and mix of transaction types. This will clearly vary from day to day and from hour to hour within each day. There may be constraints imposed by existing infrastructure such as landlines or other communication mechanisms.

6.2.3.2   Interface Functionality

The primary interfaces for this type of system are to other banks for funds transfers and use of their teller machines.

Banks also have existing systems for clearing cheques, etc. that are jointly created amongst several banks.

It is highly likely that a banking system will make use of telecommunications services from external providers.

6.2.3.3   Human Interaction Functionality

Information systems generally have to cope with a wide variety of user types. For a bank the following list covers many of them:

General public – must be able to use automatic teller machines and, increasingly, online facilities via the web without any prior training – i.e. the user interfaces must be intuitive.

Counter staff – must be able to use the system quickly in order to provide a fast and efficient service to customers queuing up. These counter staff will require training and the most important aspect of this type of interface is that it should be 'slick' when the staff have been trained.

Managers at various levels – some managers may not be quite as computer liter- ate as the counter staff (although, of course, some may have been promoted after becoming proficient as counter clerks). The facilities to be provided for the managers may include some of the counter staff facilities, but will include more summary types of information derived from looking at a wider set of information than a single account. These may include statement summaries, branch or area business summaries, etc. Note that these types of information demand that information is retained over a period of time so that trends and other historical information can be deduced and/or presented.

Policy makers and marketing staff – require quite different capabilities, perhaps introducing the capability to start new business products.

System maintainers – must be able to update system facilities. Ideally they should be able to do this while the system is fully operational, but in practice they may take down all or part of the system (usually for a brief period in the middle of the night) in order to guarantee integrity of data.

6.2.3.4   Safeguard Functionality

Security in banking systems is of paramount importance. The key element is the need to protect the integrity of the information that is at the heart of the business.

Obvious mechanisms used include the personal identification numbers (PINs) on credit or debit cards and encryption for transfers between branches, teller machines, etc.

Other areas that must be considered are the need to keep the systems working in the presence of computer faults, power failures or communication failures. These categories of functionality are related to the perception of risk. The degree of protection that can be afforded to mitigate the risks depends critically on the exposure that is perceived.

Finally and most importantly, it is necessary to consider threats from hackers, embezzlers or others with fraudulent intent. The software must provide adequate protection to safeguard the bank and its customers from these threats.

6.2.3.5   System Transactions

Each type of user is likely to be a Stakeholder in this category of system. Therefore it is likely that there will be a set of use scenarios for each type of user. For the bank customers these include regularly used facilities such as withdrawals, deposits and transfers whether made in person or done automatically as direct debits, salary payments, etc. There will also be other transactions used less frequently such as negotiating a personal loan or a mortgage.

For each type of user it is worthwhile considering the load that will be imposed, so that the response time can be estimated. Of course this will not be a fixed time, but will depend upon the current loading and this, in turn, will depend upon the time of day and day of the week.

Increasing use of web based facilities must add a further dimension to load prediction.

6.2.3.6   Modes of Operation

The predominant mode of operation will be the normal mode. However, there may be additional modes to cover training, backup and recovery operations and system evolution.

6.2.4   Car Example

The second example addresses a more physical type of system, but it is interesting to see that the same categories of information are still present, although in an entirely different form.

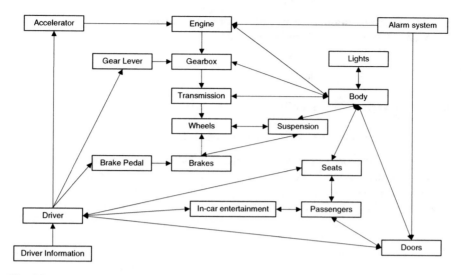

Fig. 6.7 An abstract model for a car based on physical objects

The big issue in this example is whether the system model is a physical model and to what extent it can become abstract. It is unlikely that a new car is going to be radically different in architecture from previous models – it will still have a wheel at each corner, an engine, a gearbox, suspension, a windscreen, etc. For this reason, the system model for a car may well make reference directly to the physical objects of the architecture as indicated in Fig. 6.7. The arrows on this diagram indicate "some influence" in the direction of the arrow. The driver presses the brake pedal and the brake pedal activates the brakes. The connections between the body and the parts fastened to it are shown as double ended arrows to indicate that there is a dependency in both directions, e.g. the engine is fastened to the body and the body has mountings to take the engine.

However, where aspects of the new car are likely to be rather different – such as in an electronic vehicle control system – remaining more abstract will present advantages in determining the best solution. To the extent that the functionality of a car is quite well understood, what is required is to quantify the functionality. For example, it is clear that a car must be able to move people and their luggage or other items from one place to another. The key questions that should have been addressed in the Stakeholder Requirements are:

- How many people?
- How much luggage?
- How comfortable will the car be?
- How fast will the car travel?
- How quickly will the car accelerate?
- How much will it cost?
- What information will be provided to the driver?

- What in-car entertainment facilities will be provided?
- What safety features will be necessary?
- Where will the car be used?

6.2.4.1   Internal Functionality

The key requirements that must be addressed at the functional level include:

*The acceleration rate of the car*This requires a balance between the engine power, the overall weight of the car, the wind resistance of the body and the drag induced by the wheels.

*The range of the car*This requires a balance between the fuel efficiency of the engine, the fuel capacity, whether a manual or automatic gearbox is used, and the way in which the car is driven.

*The comfort level of the car*This will influence cost and weight of the car plus people of different stature may perceive the end-result differently.

Note that these key aspects are not independent. This is typical in a systems engineering situation. It is these interactions that tend to move the model to a more abstract level. For example, the above factors will be quite different depending upon the type of engine and fuel used. Fuel types include: petroleum, diesel and liquid propane gas (LPG). The fuel efficiency and weight of engine, fuel and fuel tank are quite different in all three cases. Consequently it is necessary to determine:

- Whether to make a selection at all at this point, or
- Whether to keep all options open, or
- Whether to provide a customer selectable option for one, two or three of these types

The nature of the design will be significantly affected by the decision(s) that are taken. It may be that multiple options are evaluated, each more detailed than the overall model. Alternatively some options, for example LPG fuel, could be eliminated right at the start.

6.2.4.2   Interface Functionality

One might expect that a car is going to be isolated in terms of its need to interface with other systems. Increasingly this is not the case. One trivial example is that a car will usually have a radio receiver and this entails conforming to certain standards of demodulation in order to decode the transmitted signals.

As sophistication increases so there are wider sets of standards that must be conformed to. For example cars that have GPS navigation must understand how to receive and decode the satellite signals on which this system depends. Cars that can provide traffic information to drivers must be able to interface with the relevant information providers. In future, it is possible to envisage that the navigation system may well be influenced by the traffic information and hence a further (internal) interface will be introduced.

For modern cars, the way in which they are serviced is an important consideration. Frequently cars are required to retain information about events during their operational use so that the service technician can access it to aid in diagnosing problems or to guide him to check or change relevant items that are either faulty or nearing the end of their useful life. This is an example of a test system that is partly installed in the operational system (i.e. the car) and partly installed in the garage where the maintenance operations are undertaken.

6.2.4.3   Human Interaction Functionality

Many aspects of the 'user interface' of the car are set by conventions that have evolved over the years. For example, the relative positions of the foot pedals (accelerator on the right, brake to the left and, if present, clutch to the left of that) are identical all over the world.

Other aspects such as left-hand or right-hand drive and position of indicators and windscreen wipers have local conventions in different geographical areas.

On the other hand for entertainment systems, navigation systems and other less common systems there is, as yet, no agreed conventions and therefore the designers are free to provide an interface of their choice. As with most electronic systems, there is a need to make the interface easy to use (or even possible to use) for anybody who needs to use it. This is quite a challenge, because the only explanation that can be provided is a user guide. It is not possible to send drivers and passengers on training courses and it is not appropriate to make any assumptions about the educational level or experience of those who may need to use it.

6.2.4.4   Safeguard Functionality

The primary safeguard functionality in cars is to ensure the safety of the car and its occupants. A further, increasingly important area of functionality is the prevention of theft.

Safety functionality starts with the braking system. It is essential that effective braking is available to the driver at all times. Dual circuit hydraulic brakes that provide redundancy such that braking is still provided after any single hydraulic failure is one way of providing this. The system model could include the implementation directly; alternatively the model could just include the need for braking. In the latter case, the fact that braking must still be available in the event of a single hydraulic failure must be added outside of the model.

Note that this discussion has tacitly assumed that braking will be effected using hydraulics! Some aspects of detailed design can be included especially where there is a well-established precedent, or the decision can be taken in response to a business objective introduced into the input requirements by the developer organisation.

Other areas of safety include ABS braking and the provision of air bags to cushion the impact of a collision. Again these can either be explicitly included in the model, or the designer can be given freedom to invent alternative solutions.

The starting point for security is the provision of locks on doors. This can be enhanced by the provision of an alarm system and engine immobiliser. The limiting factor here is the cost of introducing the extra functionality and the amount that a customer is prepared to pay for it. However, there are other factors such as the facilities provided by competing cars and the attitude of insurance companies. Both have a strong influence not only on the functionality that must be provided, but also on the way its inclusion is justified.

6.2.4.5   System Transactions

There are many possible transactions for a car. All are based on journeys but with specific objectives or characteristics, for example:

- Driver, shopping trip in town – leave parking bay, travel, park, secure vehicle, unlock vehicle, load vehicle, leave parking bay, travel, park, unload, secure vehicle.
- Driver, motorway trip.
- Driver, airport trip (with luggage).
- Driver, trip with accident.
- Passenger – get in, fit belt, travel, undo belt, get out.
- Garage technician – repeatedly service, with major/minor intervals.
- Owner – buy, depreciate, sell/dispose.
- Salesman – repeatedly attempt to sell, ended by selling, warranty period.

Each of these may add new requirements such as luggage capacity or maintenance facilities.

Therefore it is important to consider them all and understand how the implied requirements of each are addressed. Of course this does not mean that all of them will be satisfied. It may be that some are rejected because they are too expensive or are not considered to be relevant for the market being considered. Alternatively the transactions may cause different models to be created for different markets.

6.2.4.6   Modes of Operation

One could imagine a car in which the prevailing terrain could influence the way in which the car operates. For example in mountainous terrain, the gearbox could automatically select lower ratios and the engine management system would take into account the amount of oxygen in the air and consequently alter the mixture of petrol and air to take account of this. Alternatively, these could be options that could be selected either at the time of purchase or when driving.

A further important mode of operation is the maintenance mode, in which the engine management system is downloading the collected information for analysis by the maintenance system and technician.

A more extreme mode could be to join a motorway "train" composed of a set of cars all travelling at the same speed with minimal spacing. The cars would then be controlled as a group and local driving facilities would be disabled.

6.2.5   Deriving Requirements from a System Model

6.2.5.1   Create a Document Structure for the Requirements

As indicated earlier, the system model may be composed of many independent and potentially overlapping models. It is possible to start deriving requirements from any of these models as has already been alluded to in the previous sections covering the banking and car examples. However, the challenge is to find a structure into which all of these derived requirements can be placed such that every requirement has an obvious place in that structure and that any empty sections are empty by design rather than by accident. The structure is referred to as a 'document structure' in Chapter 4.

It is recommended that one of the models be chosen as the primary source for generating the document structure. The model selected should be the one with the widest scope, since the system requirements must cover the complete system and not one small area. In practice the decision is usually obvious. For data oriented systems such as the banking example, the data model is often the best focus, since every function is concerned, to some extent, with establishing, disseminating, updating or safeguarding the data. For more physical systems such as the car example, it is often best to use a model derived from the physical structure of the system (assuming one exists), because most of the requirements refer to one or more of these elements.

6.2.5.2   Derive or Allocate Requirements

Once the structure has been agreed it is possible to collect all the requirements that have been derived and to place them in the structure. It may be possible to allocate some input requirements directly to the document structure. Where this is the case, it frequently means that the input requirements are too detailed i.e. too close to the implementation.

All the rules for writing good requirements outlined in Chapter 4 should be observed when formulating requirements. Remember that the golden rule is to write each requirement as a single testable statement. As each requirement is formulated it is necessary to establish traceability back to the one or more input requirements that the newly derived requirement satisfies wholly or partially.

When considering testability it may be worthwhile thinking about the criteria that will determine whether a test is considered successful or not. These acceptance criteria should be documented with each requirement. Sometimes the criteria can be embodied as a performance clause within the text of the requirement. An alternative is to write the criteria in a separate attribute alongside the requirement.

As testability and performance are being considered, it is a vital to consider how the testing, or other demonstration of successful implementation, will be organised. This leads naturally into the issue of qualification strategy and the identification, in outline, of the set of trials tests and inspections that will be necessary.

In this context it is also essential to consider the test harnesses or special test equipment that will be required. These may require separate development and, in some cases, can become separate projects in their own right. A further consideration in this area is the notion of built-in tests and the provision of monitor points. Built-in tests are increasingly important, especially in safety related area. For example, in the car example, most electronic systems will have a built-in test that is performed when the car engine is started up. Monitor points are places where significant information can be made available that would otherwise not be visible. A simple example of this is an oil pressure gauge on cars. An information example for the banking system could be a display screen showing the current transaction rates across the whole of the banking network.

The final set of requirements that should be considered is the set of constraints. These add no additional functionality, but control the way in which the functionality is delivered. At the systems requirements level, there may be some constraints that come straight from the stakeholder requirements. For example the space that a system can occupy may be limited or the stakeholders may have insisted that a pre-existing system is used as a subsystem in the new system.

Some other sources of constraint are:

Design *decisions* – e.g. the decision to have dual hydraulically operated braking system.
The application *itself* – e.g. that the equipment must be able to cope with the vibration generated by the car when it is in motion.
Safety – e.g. how can the developers convince the authorities that the car will not constitute a hazard to other road users?
Manufacturing – e.g. can the car be manufactured using the existing facilities at a reasonable cost?

6.2.6 Agreeing the System Requirements with the Design Team

The final step in the creation of the system requirements is to agree the requirements with the team who will be responsible for developing the design. This uses the agreement process described in Chapter 2 and therefore no further explanation is necessary.

6.3   Engineering Requirements from System Requirements to Subsystems

The logical next step on from the creation of the system requirements is to produce a design architecture whose components are the major subsystems of the proposed system as shown in Fig. 6.8. As usual the process starts off by agreeing the input requirements with the customer. The review criteria for system requirements must be used as the basis for the agreement process together with the general criteria presented in Chapters 2 and 4. The requirements should be free from implementation bias unless there is a specific need to constrain the design. In the latter case the requirement must be explicitly stated as a constraint. All too frequently constraints are assumed because "that is what the customer asked for". It is always good practice to challenge any design constraint, especially if the constraint is implied rather than explicit. Sometimes requirements are expressed in design terms due to laziness and because engineers have a tendency to go into too much detail too soon.

The analysis work necessary to support the agreement process helps to educate the designers about what is intended and starts them thinking about possible solutions,

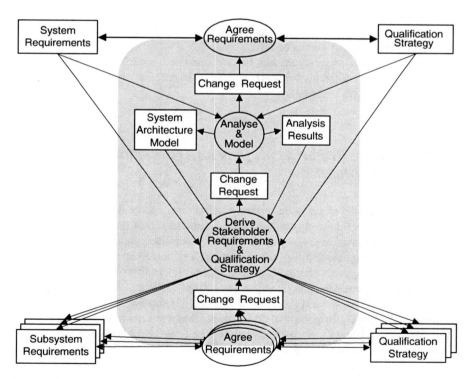

Fig. 6.8 Instantiation of generic process to create subsystem requirements from system requirements

6.3.1   Creating a System Architecture Model

An architecture model identifies the components of the system and the way in which they interact. The designer must understand how the components work together to develop the emergent properties of the system, i.e. to indicate how they satisfy the input requirements. The designers must also be able to predict whether there are any emergent properties that are definitely not required, such as catastrophic failures or other safety or environmental hazards. There may, however, be emergent properties that a given design generates that, although not actually requested by the customer, may be perfectly acceptable. These additional capabilities must be discussed with the customer. They may give rise to changes in the input requirements to request them, or the customer may request that they are inhibited. Finally the designers may find that it is impossible to satisfy the requirements at all or at reasonable cost.

It is only when a design architecture has been generated and explored that these possibilities come to light. Once a design exists it is possible to predict the cost and development time for a system with much greater accuracy than earlier. Thus it is possible to enter a round of negotiation with the customer to hone the input requirements by the customer making concessions where problems or cost dictate the need.

In many circumstances it is worthwhile considering two or more alternative designs and then investigating the relative merits of each. Again this can lead to further negotiation (trade-off) with the customer to determine the most appropriate options in terms of cost versus benefit.

When an agreed architecture has been established, each component must be described in terms of its internal functions and its interaction obligations with other components and with external systems.

6.3.2   Deriving Requirements from an Architectural Design Model

From the descriptions of the components, requirements can be derived. The requirements must address the functionality that the component must provide, the interfaces that it must use or provide and any constraints to which the component must conform. These constraints may come directly from the overall system constraints (e.g. a particular electronic technology must be used for all components), or they may be derived from them (e.g. the overall weight limit for the system has been divided amongst the components). The component (i.e. subsystem) requirements are essentially the system requirements for that component when it is viewed as a system in its own right.

As each requirement is derived, so it should be traced back to one or more of the input requirements that it partially or fully satisfies.

The strategy for testing each component must also be determined. This will not be the first occasion that testability has been considered. Testability is one of the most important aspects of the design and must be considered as the design is being created.

6.4 Other Transformations Using a Design Architecture

As the development proceeds from one level down to lower levels so each level introduces its own architectural design model (see Fig. 6.1). At each level the process followed is as described in the previous section. Thus the next level down from the creation of subsystems is to create the components of each subsystem and so on.

There is one special case in which an architectural model is used that is an exception to this rule. This is indicated in Fig. 6.9, which shows that a design architecture and subsequently subsystem requirements are created directly from the stakeholder requirements. This is only possible where the system architecture model is known in advance. Examples of this include some of the physical systems already considered, e.g. cars and aeroplanes. Another important group of applications are those in the telecommunications industry. Here the overall design architecture is mandated in the telecommunications standards that govern the application domains. It is a moot point whether the input requirements to such a process which are often taken directly from the standard are really stakeholder requirements or are, in fact, system requirements. Whatever interpretation is placed upon these requirements, during the transformation it is usual to make quite

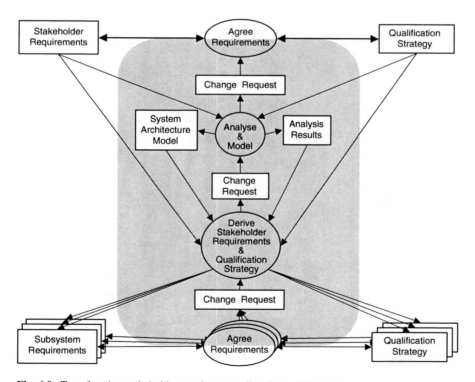

Fig. 6.9 Transforming stakeholder requirements directly to subsystems

direct allocations from the input requirements to the subsystem requirements. Again this suggests that such standards are providing requirements at quite a detailed level.

6.5 Summary

In this chapter, the nature of the solution domain has been described, the way in which requirement engineering is applied to transform stakeholder requirements to system requirements and thence to subsystem requirements and components requirements has been explained.

Two quite different examples have been used to explore the types of functionality that must be used to define requirements in the solution domain. It has been shown that, in addition to the required internal functionality, additional functionality must be added to cope with external cooperating systems, human interactions, to safeguard the system from external threatening systems make the system safe to use. The latter aspect may also involve additional constraints on the means of qualification in order to convince the relevant authorities.

Chapter 7
Advanced Traceability

For starters I'll have 'Who?', 'What?', 'When?', 'Where?',
and then 'Wither?', 'Whence?' and 'Wherefore?' to follow,
and one big side order of 'Why?'

Zaphod Beeblebrox in *The Hitch-Hiker's Guide to the Galaxy*
Douglas Noel Adams, writer, 1952–2001 AD

7.1 Introduction

So often, the real rationale for a particular design, and the deeper understanding of how the components of a system work together to achieve an end result, remain in the minds of the engineers. Months or years later, when the original designers have long since moved on, or their memory has dimmed, the loss of that understanding may seriously impede the ability to evolve, maintain or reuse the system.

This chapter first presents a technique for maintaining this greater understanding of a system, through capturing the rationale associated with the relationships between problem, solution and design. Christened "rich traceability", the approach builds on the basic concepts of "elementary traceability" presented in Chapter 1 and applied in subsequent chapters.

While rich traceability may represent one big side order of 'Why?', the 'Wither?', 'Whence?' and 'Wherefore?' of traceability are perhaps addressed through another subject of this chapter: metrics in relation to traceability.

7.2 Elementary Traceability

There are many ways of representing many-to-many relationships. One consultant visited a defence contractor just prior to a customer traceability audit to find the office all laid out ready. Along the length of the floor on one side was spread out the requirements document, and on the other side the code listing. Traceability was shown

E. Hull et al., *Requirements Engineering*, DOI 10.1007/978-1-84996-405-0_7,
© Springer-Verlag London Limited 2011

by pieces of string taped between the documents. This approach was space-consuming, time-consuming, non-maintainable, and non-transportable, but it did some of the job.

Many engineers will have seen traceability represented in matrix form as an appendix to relevant documents. The two dimensions identify, for instance, user requirements on one axis and system requirements on the other, with marks in those cells where a relationship exists.

There are a number of disadvantages to this approach:

- Where there are a large number of statements to index on both axes, the paper or screen is too small to show enough information.
- Traceability relationships tend to be sparse, resulting in most of the cells in the matrix being empty, which is a waste of space.
- It is very hard working your way through multiple layers of traceability presented in a number of separate matrices.
- Information about traceability is separated from the details of the requirements themselves.

Another method is to use hyper-linked documents, where statements can be highlighted, linked to other statements, and traversed at will – in either direction if you are clever. Now the traceability information is visible in the text of the statement, but there are still problems:

- To carry out analysis you may have physically to traverse the link before text at the other end is visible.
- It is hard to spot when the item at the other end of a hyperlink has been deleted, leaving a dangling link, making traceability difficult to maintain.

Whatever approach you use, unless supported by a tool, traceability will be very hard to manage.

The simplest form of traceability is achieved by linking statements together using some kind of database support. It is helpful if linking information is held separately from the documents. It is essential that statements are independently and uniquely identifiable.

With analysis in mind, the essential capabilities for implementation of traceability are:

- Ability to create links between statements, thus forming permitted relationships.
- Ability to delete links between statements in a controlled manner.
- Ability to view simultaneously the text (or other attributes) of statements at both ends of a selected relationship.
- Ability to carry out coverage analysis to show those statements covered or not covered by a selected relationship.
- Ability to carry out single-level and multi-level impact analysis to show sets of impacted statements.
- Ability to carry out single-level and multi-level derivation analysis to show sets of originating statements.
- Ability to carry out upwards and downwards coverage analysis to show sets of statements covered and not covered by selected relationships.

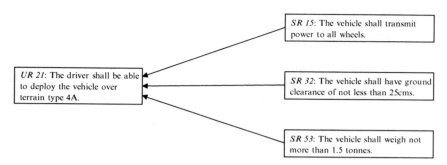

Fig. 7.1 Elementary traceability example: military vehicle

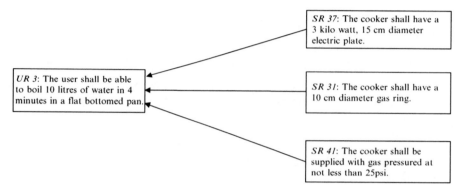

Fig. 7.2 Elementary traceability example: cooker

Figure 7.1 shows an example of elementary traceability. A user requirement traces down to three responding system requirements. In this presentation, the text of the user requirement is visible together with the set of system requirements that respond to it. Having this information together allows the traceability to be reviewed easily. Figure 7.2 shows a second example.

7.3   Satisfaction Arguments

Implementation of elementary traceability as discussed in Section 1.2 represents a major step forward for many organisations. Indeed, changing the culture of an organisation to embrace even this simple approach may be a big enough leap in itself. However, there is, as always, more that can be done.

The intention in the example of Fig. 7.1 is that the three system requirements are somehow sufficient to satisfy the user requirement. It is difficult, however, for a non-expert to assess the validity of this assertion. This is because the reasoning has not been presented.

What is better is to present a "satisfaction argument" for each user requirement. With the elementary traceability of Fig. 7.1, the only information provided is that the three system requirements play some kind of role in the satisfaction argument, but there is nothing to indicate exactly what the argument is.

Rich traceability is a way of capturing the satisfaction argument. This appears as another statement sitting between the user requirement and the corresponding system requirements, as illustrated in Fig. 7.3.

Not only is the satisfaction argument expressed textually, but an indication is given about the way in which the system requirements combine in the argument using a propositional operator:

- By conjunction (&) indicating that the contribution of *all* the system require-ments is necessary for the user requirement satisfaction argument to hold.
- By disjunction (or) indicating that the contribution of *any one of* the system requirements is necessary for the user requirement satisfaction argument to hold.

An example of disjunction is given in Fig. 7.4, where satisfaction is achieved through provision of *either* an electric ring *or* a gas ring *or both*. Note the two-level propositional structure of the argument.

Much more information is now provided about how the user requirements are being satisfied. Even one who is not a domain expert may feel capable of assessing important aspects of the argument. The text helps in assessing the logic of the argument for validity and completeness. The operator makes the structure of the argument more precise.

Notice in particular, it is not at all clear in Fig. 7.2 that the set of system requirements represent alternative solutions, whereas in Fig. 7.4 the fact is

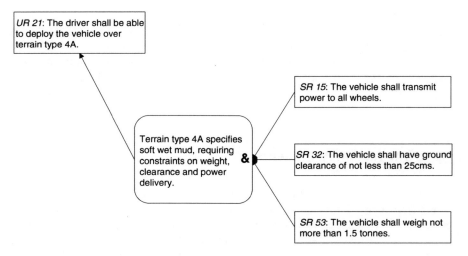

Fig. 7.3 Rich traceability example: vehicle

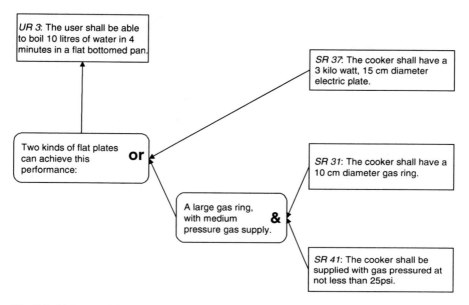

Fig. 7.4 Rich traceability example: cooker

made absolutely specific. If an electric ring cannot be supplied, the requirement can still be satisfied through a gas ring.

The authors first came across the concept of rich traceability in the Network Rail (then Railtrack) West Coast Route Modernisation project in the UK, where a team from Praxis Critical Systems had devised a requirements management process and data model that used "design justifications". The same concept can be identified in a variety of similar approaches in which satisfaction arguments are called variously "requirements elaboration", "traceability rationale", "strategy", etc.

Satisfaction arguments may depend for their validity on things other than lower-level requirements. Figure 7.5 shows an example using "domain knowledge" to support the argument. Domain knowledge is a fact or assumption about the real world, and not something that constrains the solution in and of itself. In this case, the statement of domain knowledge is an essential part of the satisfaction argument, shown in a slanted box.

Capturing such assumptions is important, not least because the world, and the assumptions you can make about it, has a habit of changing. Once captured, derivation analysis can be used to understand the impact of changing assumptions on the ability of the system to meet its requirements.

An example of this comes from the New York underground. A series of accidents in the 1970s were due to a false assumption concerning the stopping distance of trains. Initially valid, the assumption was invalidated as trains got heavier over the years, and the stopping distance increased. Whilst the performance of the signalling software was originally correct, and it did not evolve, the changing assumptions meant that it ceased to meet requirements from a certain time.

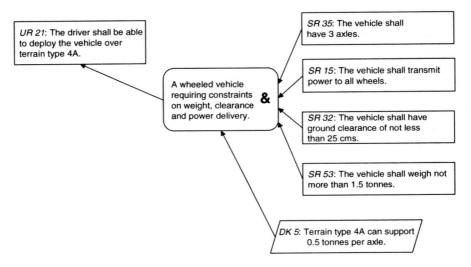

Fig. 7.5 The role of domain knowledge

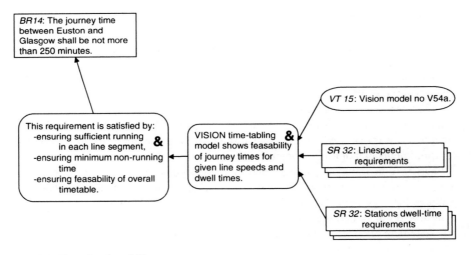

Fig. 7.6 The role of modelling

The ability to document and trace the role of such assumptions is possible through effective traceability.

Another example of non-requirements information playing a role in satisfaction arguments comes from modelling activities. Satisfaction arguments are often derived from complex modelling activities, the complete details of which are too detailed to be captured in rich traceability.

Figure 7.6 shows an example abstracted from a railway project in which a satisfaction argument depends on the results of a complex timetable modelling

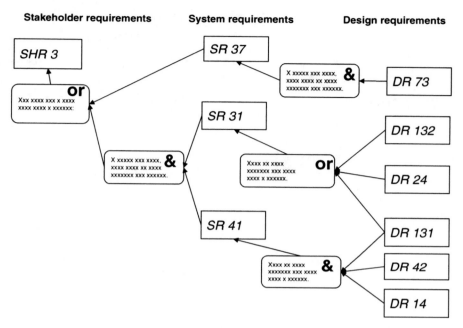

Fig. 7.7 Multiple layers of rich traceability

activity using specialised software. A set of assumptions and subsystem requirements are derived from the modelling tool, and these are documented in the rich
traceability structure. The modelling reference is shown in a box with rounded
ends.

In this case, the modelling activities that need revisiting become apparent under
impact analysis.

Rich traceability can of course be used through multiple layers of requirements
or objectives. Figure 7.7 depicts three layers and the traceability between them.

7.4 Requirements Allocation

The satisfaction argument is often trivial, amounting perhaps only to the allocation
of an identical requirement to one or more subsystems or components. This is
sometimes referred to as requirements "allocation" or "flow-down".

Where this pure flow-down of requirements is used, the change process may be
simplified. Changes to high-level requirements may be automatically flowed-down
to lower levels.

A simple extension of rich traceability allows such cases to be captured. A new
value representing "identity" is added to the "and" and "or" operators used to annotate the arguments. Figure 7.8 shows an example of this. The symbol "=" is used to
indicate identity.

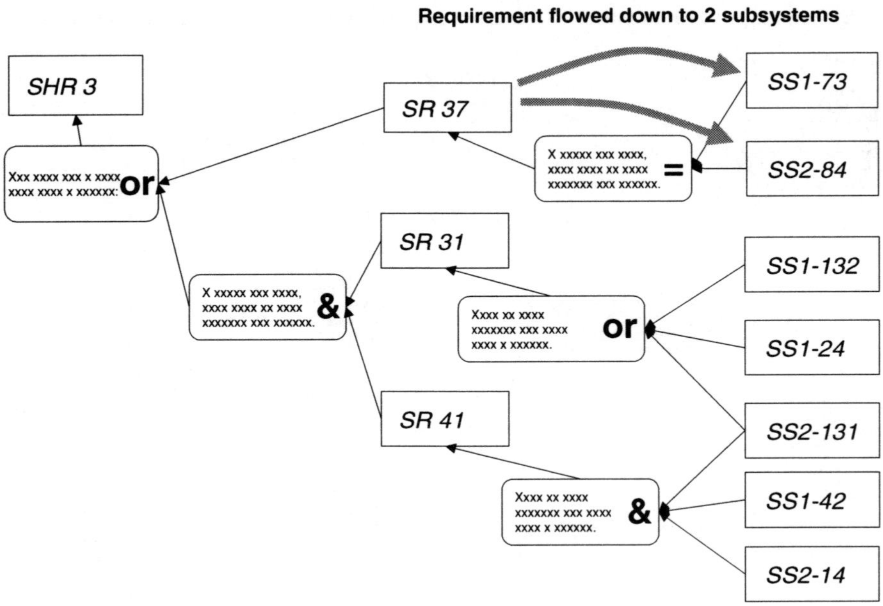

Requirement flowed down to 2 subsystems

Fig. 7.8 Flow-down of requirements using "identity"

7.5 Reviewing Traceability

Every time a requirement is reviewed, it should be reviewed along with its satisfaction argument. Based on rich traceability, a review process can be established that focuses on one requirement at a time, together with its satisfaction argument, and the requirements that flow from it.

Figure 7.9 shows a screen shot of a tool used in a defence project to review requirements and satisfaction arguments. On the screen is just the right parcel of information to assess a requirement and how it is satisfied.

The dark triangles are for navigating downwards through the layers of traceability, or across to the next requirement at the same level.

7.6 The Language of Satisfaction Arguments

As with requirements, it helps to have a uniform approach to expressing satisfaction arguments. The key guideline is to start the sentence with "This requirement will be satisfied by ...", which focuses the mind on the kind of statement being made.

While requirements should be strictly atomic (see Chapter 4), satisfaction arguments need not be so limited. However, if statements become too complex, a structured argument should be used instead.

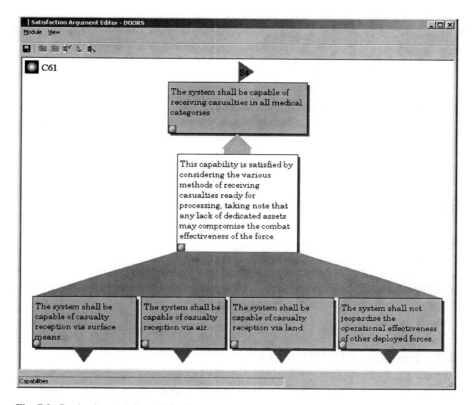

Fig. 7.9 Reviewing tool for satisfaction arguments

Repeated patterns of satisfaction arguments may be identifiable, in which case a palette of boilerplate statements could be used to good effect.

7.7 Rich Traceability Analysis

The presence of satisfaction arguments in rich traceability does not preclude the ability to carry out elementary impact and derivation analysis as described in Chapter 1. Indeed, the arguments add important clues as to the nature of the impact by capturing understanding, or *raison-d'être*.

The propositional structure (and's and or's) of the satisfaction arguments offers opportunities for other kinds of analysis. For instance, the structures can be analysed to show the number of degrees of freedom that exist for meeting a particular objective.

Take the example of Fig. 7.4. The proposition structure for *UR3* can be captured in the expression SR37 *or (SR31 and SR41)*. Using the laws of propositional logic, this can be converted to a special disjunctive form in which each disjunct shows one way of meeting the requirement:

[SR37 and (not SR31) and (not SR41)]
or [SR37 and SR31 and (not SR41)]
or [SR37 and (not SR31) and SR41]
or [SR37 and SR31 and SR41]
or [(not SR37) and SR31 and SR41]

In simple cases, this analysis may not seem that useful, but imagine more complex scenarios where there are hundreds of requirements in several layers with complex interactions. One may want to know whether there is *any* way of meeting the requirements, and if there is no way, then what the cause is – where the conflict exists.

7.8   Rich Traceability for Qualification

Rich traceability can be used in any traceability relationship. The discussion so far has been based on the satisfaction relationship, but it is also applicable to qualification. In this case, the "satisfaction argument" may be referred to as the "qualification argument" or "qualification rationale". All the same advantages of using satisfaction arguments apply to the qualification strategy.

7.9   Implementing Rich Traceability

We describe here two approaches to the implementation of rich traceability: single-layer and multi-layer.

7.9.1   Single-Layer Rich Traceability

In this approach, illustrated in Fig. 7.10, each high-level requirement has a single statement of satisfaction or strategy as an attribute, and multiple low-level requirements

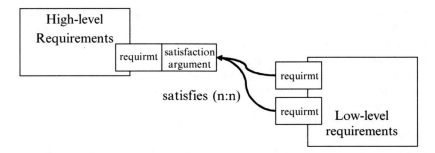

Fig. 7.10 Single-layer rich traceability

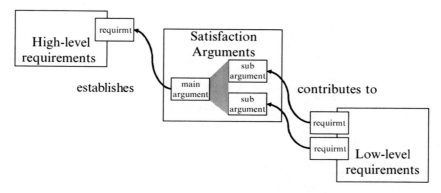

Fig. 7.11 Multi-layer rich traceability

may flow from it in a many-to-many satisfaction relationship. Another attribute (not shown in the diagram) is used to type the argument as either a conjunction or a disjunction.

7.9.2 Multi-Layer Rich Traceability

Here satisfaction arguments can be structured into multiple layers: a main argument attached (as an attribute or linked in an "establishes" relationship) to the requirement to be established, and a hierarchy of sub-arguments hang off of the main argument. Low-level requirements are linked to the sub-arguments in a "contributes to" relationship. This is shown in Fig. 7.11.

Some implementations limit the depth of the argument hierarchy to two, using a main argument – the satisfaction argument – and a single layer of sub-arguments that explains the role played by the contributing requirements.

7.10 Design Documents

Astute readers will have noticed that the layer of rationale introduced by satisfaction arguments is very like the "filling" in the systems engineering sandwich presented in Fig. 1.9. Indeed, the satisfaction arguments can be gathered into a document, which may be best characterised as an "analysis and design" document. It is this design document which is the focal point of the integration between requirements and modelling. The role of the design document is to summarize – textually and visually – those parts of the modelling activity that explain why one layer of requirements is sufficient and necessary to satisfy the layer above. The document references data from the modelling process as evidence for the rationale. Traceability between layers of requirement passes through the design document.

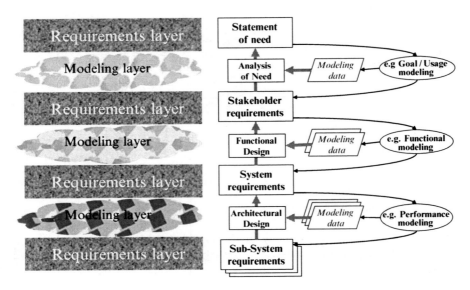

Fig. 7.12 Analysis and design documents

In this way, the results of modelling appear in the traceability chain, and can engage in impact analysis.

Figure 7.12 portrays this approach. Layers of requirements are filled by design documents appropriate to the level of abstraction. The modelling activities at each level give rise to data that is referenced by the design document. The thin arrows represent the flow of information; the thick arrows represent traceability.

We now show an example of the kind of information that may be collected into a design document. A sequence of figures shows extracts from an "Analysis of Need" document that models a Baggage Check-in System at the problem domain level. The model sits between the "Statement of Need" and the "Stakeholder Requirements" documents, and uses UML2 to portray the analysis in visual form.

The following kinds of information are typical:

- *Concepts*   A UML class diagram is used to identify the domain concepts and the relationships between them. Each concept is a UML class, and each relationship is a UML association. Both appear as entries in the design document where a textual description of the concept or relationship is supplied. Figure 7.13 shows an example for the Baggage Check-in System. The symbols to the left of each paragraph indicate that that part of the document corresponds to a UML entity in the model.
- *Stakeholders*   This section lists the stakeholders that have been identified during analysis, and includes a class diagram showing relationships. In the example shown in Fig. 7.14, there are two stakeholders with a single relationship.
- *Static Context*   The purpose of this section is to identify the context in which the Baggage Check-in System exists. The Baggage Check-in System itself is

1 Concepts

This section will contain textual descriptions of the following modelling entities. Each one will correspond to a "Class" in the UML model.

1.1 Baggage Item

The term 'Baggage Item' refers to a single item of luggage.
Each passenger may have 0 or more items of luggage.

1.2 Trackable Baggage Item

The term 'Trackable Baggage' refers to a Baggage Item that can be identified with a particular passenger.

1.3 Baggage Receipt

The term 'Baggage Receipt' refers to a means of allowing a passenger to assert ownership of an item of baggage.

1.3.1 identifies

A Baggage Receipt serves to uniquely identify a Baggage Item.

1.4 Concept Relationships

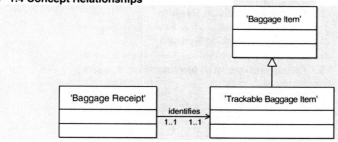

Fig. 7.13 Concepts section of design document

3 Stakeholders

This section will contain textual descriptions of each kind of stakeholder. Each one should correspond to an "Actor" in the UML model.

3.1 Passenger

A passenger is any person wishing to travel on a flight.

3.2 Family

A family is a group of passengers travelling together. They may share luggage, and wish to sit together.

3.3 Stakeholder Relationships

Optional class diagram showing sub-type relationships between stakeholders, if any.

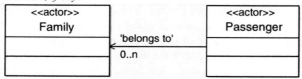

Fig. 7.14 Stakeholders section of design document

3 Context

Start with a class diagram that shows the significant context of the system to be developed.

3.1 Baggage Check-in System

This section identifies and introduces the system to be developed.

3.2 Baggage Handling System

This is the enclosing system. (Concept of system-of-systems.)
It must be a class, so that an architexture diagram can be drawn for it, but we stereotype it as an actor.

3.3 Baggage Transport System

This is a peer system, so we make it a class, but stereotype it as an actor.

3.4 Passenger Transport System

This is a peer system, so we make it a class, but stereotype it as an actor.

3.5 Baggage Reclaim System

This is a peer system, so we make it a class, but stereotype it as an actor.

3.6 Baggage Holding System

This is a peer system, so we make it a class, but stereotype it as an actor.

3.7 Relationships with surrounding systems

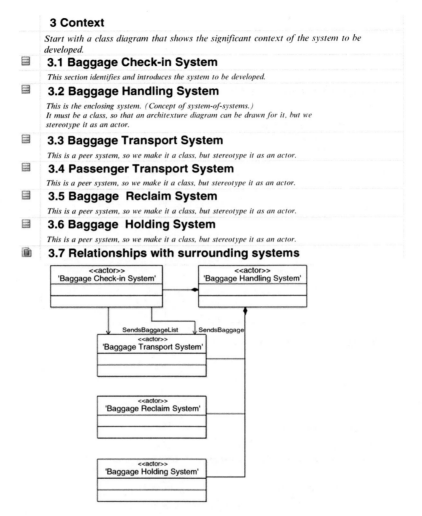

Fig. 7.15 Context section of design document

modeled as a class in a class diagram, along with classes representing all the surrounding and enclosing systems. Relationships between these systems are modeled using aggregations and associations. Again, each class and association appears in the design document with a textual description (Fig. 7.15).

- *Usage* This section describes the top level use cases for the system. This is presented as a series of use case diagrams, each with one or more sequence diagrams. Figure 7.16 shows just one of the use cases and its sequence diagram showing the normal course of action for the scenario. The sequence diagram shows the interactions between the stakeholders (some of which are external subsystems) and the system in question (the Baggage Check-in System), and thus helps to define the scope, process context and external interfaces.

4 Usage Context

Here we give top-level use cases.

4.1 Travel with Baggage

General description of use case.

4.1.1 Use Case

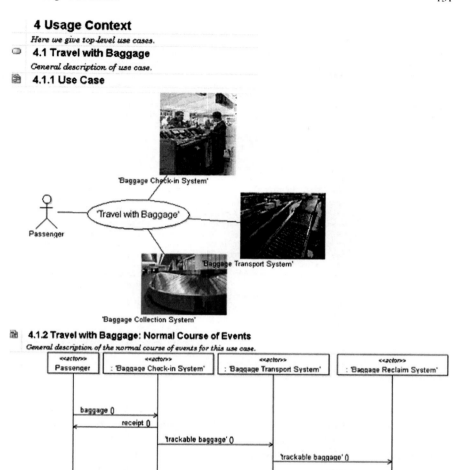

4.1.2 Travel with Baggage: Normal Course of Events

General description of the normal course of events for this use case.

Fig. 7.16 Usage section of design document

- *Design rationale* This section summarizes the analysis and modeling activity by giving an explanation of how the need is going to be satisfied by the capabilities of the system. One way of presenting this information is in the form of a "satisfaction argument" for each statement in the input requirements document. It is here that the traceability to high-level requirements and from low-level requirements is established. The satisfaction argument, in effect, explains how the statement of need has been decomposed into statements of capability. This is illustrated in Fig. 7.17.

1 Design Rationale

1.1 Reduce check-in time

[SoN-9] Passengers will be able to check-in baggage on average twice as fast as the current average for given number of items. The current average is 80 secs per item.	This objective will be met by ensuring that the Baggage Check-in System has sufficient performance at the point of check-in. A separation will be made between the check. in of the passenger and the check-in of that passenger's baggage. The target check-in for each item of baggage is 25 seconds. This strategy is reflected in the following ways: • passenger check-in and baggage item check-in are separate events in the modeled scenarios; • a performance requirement is imposed on the baggage check-in capability.	*[PA-233] UML Sequence diagram* Travel With Baggage: Normal Course of Events *[SHR-3]* At the port of departure, the passenger shall be able to check-in an item of baggage within 25 seconds of placing it on the conveyor.

1.2 Increase security standards

Baggage Item

[SoN-8] Passengers will only be allowed to collect baggage that they themselves checked-in on departure.	This objective will be met by issuing unique receipts to passengers for baggage check-in on departure, allowing trackable baggage to be matched with those receipts, and obliging passengers to present those receipts to the Baggage Collection System on arrival. This strategy is reflected in the following ways: • a distinction is made between baggage and trackable baggage; • every item of trackable baggage has a unique receipt; • presentation of receipts by passengers occurs at baggage collection.	*[PA-3]* The term 'Baggage Item' refers to a single item of luggage. **Trackable Baggage Item** *[PA-6]* The term 'Trackable Baggage' refers to a Baggage Item that can be identified with a particular passenger. **identifies** *[PA-263]* A Baggage Receipt serves to uniquely identify a Baggage Item. *[PA-233] UML Sequence diagram* Travel with Baggage: Normal Course of Events *[SHR-5]* At the port of arrival, the passenger shall be able to collect baggage he/she checked-in on departure.

Fig. 7.17 Rationale section of design document

In this figure, the first column shows the text of the Statement of Need that is addressed by the rationale, the middle column contains the rationale, and the right-hand column shows evidence for the rationale in the model and requirements that are derived from it. This tabular presentation is, in effect, the sandwich on its side: two layers of requirement with the design rationale in between. With effective tool support, this view of the project data can be generated from the presence of tracing between the layers.

7.11 Metrics for Traceability

Since the concept of traceability is so central to requirements engineering, it is interesting to consider what process measurements may be useful in relation to the flow-down of requirements.

Focussing on the satisfaction relationship, and moving down through the layers of requirements, there are three dimensions of traceability that may interest us:

Breadth: how well does the relationship cover the layer, upwards and downwards?

Depth: how far down (or up) the layers does the relationship extend?

Growth: how much does the relationship expand down through the layers?

To help in determining which aspects of these dimensions are useful in terms of measuring the requirements engineering process, it is necessary to distinguish between two types of metrics:

Phase metrics: measurements relating to a single stage of development, e.g. just to the systems requirements layer;

Global metrics: measurements spanning several stages of development.

The three dimensions, along with a discussion about balance, are now addressed.

7.11.1 Breadth

Breadth relates to coverage, and as such is a phase metric. As discussed in Chapter 1, coverage can be used to measure progress of processes that create traceability at a single stage. It focuses on a single layer, and measures the extent to which requirements are covered by the adjacent level above or below (or 'beside' when looking at qualification.)

7.11.2 Depth

Depth looks at the number of layers that traceability extends upwards or downwards from a given layer, making it a global metric. One application may relate to determining the origins of requirements of the lowest level. How many component requirements have actually flowed down all the way from the stakeholder requirements, and how many have their origin somewhere in the design?

7.11.3 Growth

Growth is more interesting. It is related to potential change impact. How many requirements at lower levels are related to a single requirement at the top level?

Consider Fig. 7.18, in which four situations are contrasted.

In case (a), a single requirement is satisfied by a single requirement at the next level down. The growth factor is 1. In (b) the single requirement is met by 6, giving a growth factor of 6. What does this say about the differences between the two requirements? Possibilities are:

Requirement (b) may be poorly expressed, and needs decomposing into several

Requirement (b) may be inherently more complex than (a), and therefore may need special attention

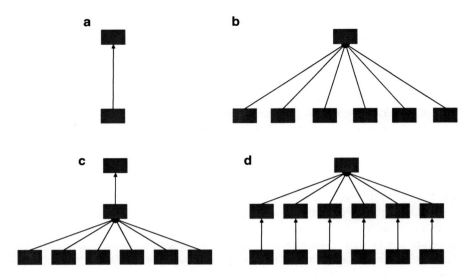

Fig. 7.18 Traceability growth

Changing requirement (b) will have more impact than changing (a), and therefore needs special attention

Of course, an apparent imbalance at one level may be addressed at the next level down. This is illustrated by cases (c) and (d), where the growth factor two levels down is identical. What could be deduced from this? Possibilities are:

- The top requirement in (c) was at a level too high.
- The middle requirements in (d) were at a level too low.

Only after considerable experience in a particular organisation developing particular kinds of systems could one begin to ascertain what growth factor of requirements between layers is to be expected. More readily useful, however, would be to examine the balance of growth between requirements, as a means of identifying potential rogue requirements, or imbalances in the application of process.

7.11.4 Balance

One idea for a metric is to look at the distribution of growth factors for individual requirements between two given layers, and examine those that lie in the outer quartiles of the distribution. The goal is to identify requirements that have an abnormally high or low growth factor, and subject them to special scrutiny.

Figure 7.19 shows what a typical growth distribution may look like. The graph plots the growth rate against the number of requirements that possess that growth rate. Most lie between 2 and 6, whereas a few have only 1 or more than 6. It is these latter requirements that should be identified and given special attention.

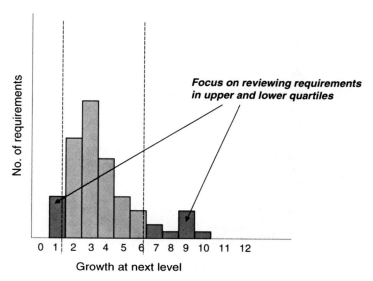

Fig. 7.19 Frequency distribution of requirement growth

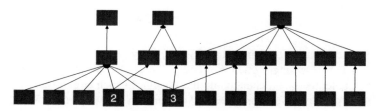

Fig. 7.20 Criticality of requirements

The discussion above was about downwards growth – examining the number of requirements that flow out of another. What about the opposite direction: the number of requirements that flow *into* another?

Bearing in mind that traceability is a many-to-many relationship, consider Fig. 7.20. Two requirements at the lower level have more than one requirement flowing into them. What can we say about these requirements? They are perhaps more critical than others, since they satisfy multiple requirements, and should therefore be given special attention.

The distribution of upward traceability can be used to single out these requirements. Figure 7.21 shows the typical shape of such a distribution.

7.11.5 Latent Change

Change management is perhaps the most complex requirements engineering process. ability to determine the potential impact of change. When a change request is raised

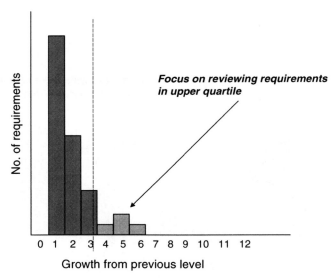

Fig. 7.21 Frequency distribution of requirement criticality

against one requirement, all those tracing to it move to a suspect status until the engineers ascertain the true impact.

The raising of a single change request, therefore, can suddenly introduce a cascade of potential latent change into the system. In such circumstances, it would be highly desirable to track progress and estimate the consequential work.

Figure 7.22 illustrates the complexity of change impact. A change request is raised on one of the highest-level requirements. Part (a) shows the potential impact using downwards traceability. Those boxes marked with a white circle are subject to change assessment.

Part (b) then shows potential change using upwards impact. This occurs because of a low-level requirement that flows down from two higher requirements. It is necessary to access upwards impact from these changes, because changes in a low-level requirement may cause renegotiation at a higher level. Suddenly *everything* in this example is potentially subject to change!

Of course, as engineers assess the real impact, it may be found that in fact some of these requirements are not subject to change after all, and the cascade of potential changes can thankfully be pruned, sometimes quite substantially.

The status of change can simply be measured in terms of the number of requirements still in a suspect state. When a change request is raised, all other requirements traceable downwards and upwards are marked as suspect. Then the number of suspect requirements will steadily decrease as assessments are made of each, their state is reset, possibly resulting in a cascade of others being reset as well. The amount of residual change in a system will thus peak every time a new change is introduced, and tail-off, as illustrated in Fig. 7.23.

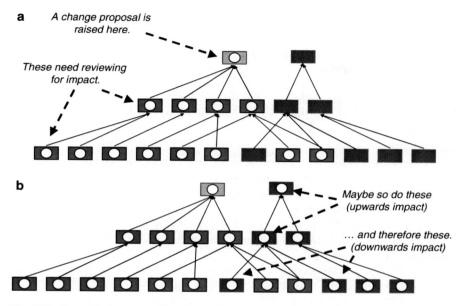

Fig. 7.22 Potential change resulting from a change request

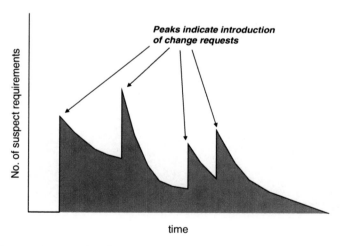

Fig. 7.23 Progress in processing change

The above discussion of the change process supposes that change is propagated from requirement to requirement purely through the *existing* set of links. However, a change in a requirement may necessitate the addition or removal of traceability links. Changes in links should propagate change to the connected requirements at both ends.

7.12 Summary

Of all the advantages in the use of traceability cited in Chapter 1, Section 1.5, it is the increase in confidence in meeting requirements that is so clearly addressed through rich traceability. The discipline of capturing the rationale associated with traceability builds that confidence.

There is no doubt that there is considerable effort involved in the creation of complete satisfaction arguments, especially in complex systems with hundreds of requirements.

In the Network Rail project, there are some 500 satisfaction arguments that serve to decompose the high-level requirements through to subsystem requirements. A team of between two and five requirements engineers was dedicated to the maintenance of this information over about 3 years.

Experience suggests, however, that the cost is amply repaid in the increased confidence that comes from the greater reflection required. The ability for the Network Rail sponsor organisation to take a high-level objective, and demonstrate in detail through the layers of rich traceability exactly how that objective is going to be met, was a major selling point for the concept.

It is clear, also, that traceability is a rich source of metrics for process measurement. It is the formalisation of relationships through traceability and associated processes that make such measurement possible.

Chapter 8
Management Aspects of Requirements Engineering

In theory there is no difference between theory and practice.
In practice there is.

Yogi Berra, baseball player, b. 1925 AD

8.1 Introduction to Management

The management of the requirements engineering process is similar to the management of any other endeavour. Before starting out it is necessary to understand what needs to be done. We need to know the sorts of activities that must be undertaken. We need to know whether there are any dependencies between the activities, e.g. whether one activity can only commence when another one has been completed. We need to know what kinds of skills are required to perform the activities.

It is good practice when preparing a plan to concentrate on the outputs that will be generated by each activity. Outputs can be seen and provide tangible evidence that work has been or is being done.

From all of this information we can generate a plan in which we have identified the activities to be undertaken, the people who will perform the activities and the time it will take them to complete the activities. We can then start work following the plan and the manager can monitor work against the plan. In an ideal world the plan will be followed to the letter. Nothing will go wrong and we shall arrive at the completion date of the plan with all the work done.

Reality can be quite different. Firstly, estimating the time and effort required to complete a task is very difficult unless the manager has extensive experience of tackling similar jobs in the past. Secondly, there may be difficulties discovered as work progresses that could not have been foreseen. For example, the plan may have relied on the availability of a key person at a specific time and, for any number of reasons, that person is not able to be there.

These events cause deviations from the plan and lead to the need to change it. Once a new plan has been put in place, the whole process is repeated. A frequent consequence of changing the plan is that, almost inevitably, the cost will increase and/or the time to completion will be later than previously estimated. An alternative

E. Hull et al., *Requirements Engineering*, DOI 10.1007/978-1-84996-405-0_8,
© Springer-Verlag London Limited 2011

Fig. 8.1 Capability, cost and
time are interrelated

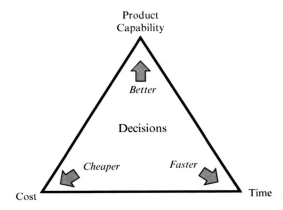

approach is to keep the costs and completion time constant and reduce the amount of work to be done. This can be a viable strategy in some circumstances; for example, it may be imperative that a company has a new product out in the market place at a given time (to address the competition) and within a given budget (because that is all the company can afford) irrespective of how capable the product is (although at least a threshold level is usually necessary to avoid triviality). This situation is typical of the way in which commercial pressures can drive a project.

It is important to recognise that any project is constrained by the three factors:

- Product capability
- Cost
- Timescale

These three factors are related as indicated in the diagram of Fig. 8.1. Any change to one of these factors will have a consequential change to at least one of the others. Figure 8.1 also indicates that projects make progress by taking decisions. Every decision positions the project with respect to these three fundamental factors. It is the pipe dream of every project manager that each decision will improve the product capability whilst simultaneously reducing cost and shortening development time. In spite of its improbability, this dream is widely held.

8.2   Requirements Management Problems

In this section introduces the specific problems that make the management of requirements more difficult than some other management activities. The first problem is that very few people have had significant experience of managing requirements. This is mainly because very few organisations have a defined requirements management process that is followed across the organisation. As a result people faced with a project that must address requirements, have very little experience to draw on. This makes estimation very difficult, because one of the main ingredients to the production of good estimates is extensive relevant experience. Thus the starting point is not good and one is reminded of the joke in which one person asks another the way to a specific place and receives the reply "I wouldn't start from here"!

A corollary of this problem is more fundamental. If people have had little experience of requirements management, they may not even know what activities are necessary to develop requirements. Earlier chapters of this book have addressed this issue and give direct guidance on the sorts of activities necessary to develop requirements of various types and in several contexts.

The second problem is that many people do not properly distinguish between user or stakeholder requirements and system requirements. Further they often do not distinguish between system requirements and design specifications. In other words they go straight for a solution rather than defining a solution-independent set of requirements. Again this topic has been dealt with in the preceding chapters of this book.

The third main problem is that the way in which requirements are managed will depend upon the type of organisation in which the work is being done. In the preceding chapters we have discussed the different types of requirements and indicated how they are related. However, the way in which these processes are applied will depend upon the type of organisation applying them. There are three main types of organisation:

- Acquisition oranisations that purchase systems and then use them to provide an operational capability. These organisations are mainly concerned with creating and managing Stakeholder requirements, which subsequently are used as the basis for acceptance of the delivered system.
- Supplier organisations that respond to acquisition requests from Acquisition organisations or higher level Supplier organisations. These organisations receive Input Requirements and develop system requirements (and subsequently a design that is manufactured) in response to them. (Suppliers may also be acquirers of lower level subsystems or components, but this is a quite different form of acquisition because it is based on a design architecture.)
- Product companies that develop and sell products. These organisations collect Stakeholder requirements but from their market place rather than from individuals or from operations organisations. The marketing department usually performs the collection of requirements. Product companies develop products in response to the stakeholder (marketing) requirements and sell the developed products. In a sense these types of organisations encompass both acquisition and supply, but they tend to have a different relationship between the parts of the company that perform these roles compared to the standard acquisition and supplier relationship.

We will return to these types of organisation later in this chapter.

The fourth problem that makes the management of requirements more difficult than some other management activities is that it is quite difficult to monitor progress when requirements are being generated. One difficult issue is to know whether the requirements set is complete – in order to decide whether the activity should stop. Even worse, is the problem of determining how much progress has been made when the activity is nowhere near completion. This problem is further exacerbated by the need to assess the quality of the requirements generated. A long list of requirements may have been generated, but how does the manager assess whether each requirement is well expressed? How can he tell whether each requirement is unique and whether they are all necessary?

The final problem is the perennial problem of changes. Requirements management should be the primary focus for change management. Any proposed change will usually relate to one or more requirements. The impact or knock-on effects of proposed changes are quite often difficult to assess, yet without this knowledge it is impossible to estimate the cost and time impact of introducing a change.

8.2.1 Summary of Requirement Management Problems

Specific management issues for requirements development arise in connection with:

- Planning
- Monitoring progress
- Controlling changes

The problems are subtly different depending on the organisation involved. Therefore, in the rest of this chapter we consider each of these activities in the context of the three types of organisations introduced earlier. Finally we draw together some common approaches in a concluding section.

8.3 Managing Requirements in an Acquisition Organisation

8.3.1 Planning

The starting point for a project in an Acquisition Organisation will be some form of concept description. In its most basic form this will be just an idea, but usually it will be more concrete and well founded. The reason for this is simple: projects must be authorised by the organisation and the authorisation process will require some documented evidence to support the case for spending time and money (resources). The evidence usually contains a brief description of what the users want to be able to do (the concept) and a supporting argument to indicate the benefits that will ensue to the operating organisation from the provision of such a capability.

The information in the concept definition enables the project manager to begin planning. Since the concept definition contains a *"description of what the users want to be able to do"* we immediately have an initial set of Stakeholders (*users*) for the system and an outline of one or more Scenarios (*ability to do something*).

The first step in constructing a plan consists of identifying a fuller set of Stakeholder types and a more complete set of Scenarios that cover the complete range of expected operation of the system including, where useful, different modes of operation. Once the number of stakeholder types is known it is possible to plan in detail how to set about eliciting requirements. Actions that may be instantiated in the plan include:

(a) Plan to interview one or more candidates of each stakeholder type. The requirements manager is responsible for ensuring that authorisation to conduct the interviews is obtained from the candidates' managers. Authorisation may depend upon appropriate job codes and budgets being agreed (so that the candidates interviewed can book their time to the new project and consequently their managers are not penalised for their staff's absence whilst being interviewed). The requirements manager should also ensure that access to key operations staff is provided. Often the candidates' managers will be unwilling to release their most competent (useful and well informed) staff for an activity that is not in their short-term interests. It is up to the requirements manager to convince them of the value of doing so.

(b) Allocate time to write up the interviews as interview reports and agree them with candidates interviewed.

(c) Decide the interview strategy and communicate to the interviewers (who may be involved in the decision process anyway). The interview strategy will determine how each interview is conducted, for example, whether candidates should be prompted to express scenarios themselves, or be presented with a suggested scenario that they can criticise, etc.

(d) Prior to the interviews it can be useful (but not necessarily easy) to get all the candidates together and explain the purpose of the interviews. If such a meeting can be arranged, it provides an excellent forum in which to discuss/develop user scenarios and to seek confirmation that all stakeholder types have been identified

(e) Agree and document the set of user scenarios that best reflect the purpose and operation of the system in its context. It is essential to ensure that the scenarios are not too blinkered in their scope.

(f) Following the interviews, suggested stakeholder requirements can be extracted from the interview reports and agreed with the interview candidates

(g) Decide on a structure into which each of the stakeholder requirements can be entered.

(h) Place each identified stakeholder requirement within the agreed structure and modify the structure as necessary.

(i) Identify and record any constraints. Some constraints are product requirements such as physical size. Others are plan constraints such as budgeted cost and completion time. The product constraints should be entered into the Stakeholder Requirements Specification. The planning constraints (such as budget, schedule, resource or quality) belong in the management plan and will have an influence on the planning activity.

(j) Decide whether additional attributes are required to support the text of the requirements. Many organisations have standard sets of attributes that may be required or are merely advisory. Examples are: Priority, Urgency, Status, Validation method, Acceptance criterion.

(k) Agree the criteria for the review of each individual requirement and for the requirement set as a whole. These criteria are best presented as a checklist for the reviewers. Ideally the review criteria should be created as early as possible and distributed to the people writing the requirements. This enables them to appreciate what is required of them before they start to write.

(l) Define the review process and relate this to the status of the individual requirements. This process can be summarised as a state transition diagram as shown in Fig. 8.2. This shows that the initial state of a stakeholder requirement is 'Proposed'. When the requirements management team has reviewed it, it can move to the Reviewed status. Reviewed requirements can then be subjected to a further review by the Sponsor's team and, when successful, will achieve Endorsed status. Note that, at any time, an Active requirement can be rejected. Review criteria must be determined for each review.

(m) Perform reviews as required by the review procedure defined.

This list of activities implies the need for several decisions to be taken. This is the requirements manager's responsibility in collaboration with other interested parties such as the interview candidates, their managers and the overall sponsor for the system.

Care should be taken to assess any planning constraints to ensure that they are feasible and sensible. Stakeholders may demand that the system is put in service in a very short period of time and at low cost, but this may not be possible. A prime example of an unrealistic time constraint comes from the London Ambulance System developed to control ambulances in London in the early 1990s. The managers wanted to have the system in place so that they could supply the government with the performance statistics they were demanding. This very short development period and early in-service date were placed on the project as overall constraints, but were absolutely impossible to meet. Many contractors tried to persuade the ambulance service that it was impossible to meet these constraints and asked for the in-service date to be put back. These requests were refused and so many contractors did not bid. This left less experienced contractors to attempt to meet the impossible constraint.

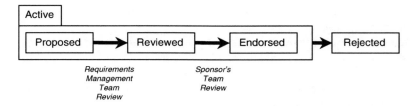

Fig. 8.2 Example state transition diagram for stakeholder requirement status

History shows that they completely failed to meet the demanded deadline and in the process caused serious harm to many people.

Realism in planning is essential for professional integrity.

8.3.2 Monitoring

Monitoring can start once the plan is in place. Obvious monitoring points are the completion of each activity in the plan. In the early stages the activities will mainly revolve around preparing for the interviews, conducting them and reporting on them. These are quite easy to assess.

Three major milestones help to define the monitoring for the rest of the process:

1. The definition of the structure for the requirements specification
2. The definition of the attributes required for each requirement
3. The definition of the review process(es) with associated checklists

Once the structure is in place it is possible to determine whether there are any areas where there should be requirements but none exist. These "holes" can be addressed by specific actions.

Once the attributes have been decided, progress in filling them can be monitored.

Finally, the progress against satisfying the review checklist criteria can be checked by measuring the number of requirements that have a specific status.

8.3.3 Changes

During the development of stakeholder requirements there will be a period of rapid and intense change. At this stage it is not sensible to have a formal change control process in place, because the situation is too dynamic and would just get in the way. However, at some point stability will begin to emerge and the requirements manager can determine when the requirements are sufficiently stable to subject further changes to a more formal process. Often this stage only occurs once all the requirements have been reviewed and reach the Endorsed state (see Fig. 8.2).

Managing change is a vital activity in requirements development. The formality with which the process must be applied depends upon the development state of the project. Important stages include the following:

- Stakeholder Requirements used as the basis for a competitive bidding process.
- Contract in place for the development of a system.
- Design complete and manufacturing about to start.
- Acceptance trials are being undertaken.
- The system is in service.

This list defines a set of points in a sequence of increasing commitment. Hence the further down this list a project is, the more formality is required in the change control process and the higher the likely cost impact of any change.

Whatever stage a project is at, the following steps are required in a change control process:

1. Record the suggested change
2. Identify the impact of the suggested change
3. Decide whether to accept the change
4. Decide when to implement the change

The suggested change should indicate the reason for the change and identify the stakeholder requirements that must be changed, added or deleted. The person or organisation requesting the change must also be recorded.

At step 2 the impact will depend upon the stage at which the change is suggested and this will require information about how the impacted requirements will influence the downstream information such as system requirements, design, manufacturing and in-service operations.

A Change Control Board will take step 3. The constitution of this board will depend upon the organisation, the scale of the system, and the stage of development or operational use of the system. If a change is accepted, then step 4 is required. It may be that the change must be incorporated immediately irrespective of cost. Alternatively the change may be deferred until a later release of the system. Any number of intermediate points may be appropriate and this clearly depends on circumstances.

It is always useful to have a set of states for a change and to represent this using a state transition diagram or statechart. Figure 8.3 contains an example.

It is also important to decide whether the status of requirements that are the subject of a change proposal should be changed to indicate this. There are at least two schools of thought on this point. One group takes the view that the dependency

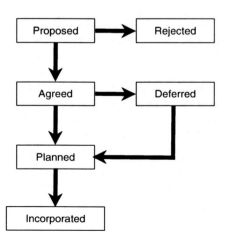

Fig. 8.3 State transition diagram for change control

between the change and the requirements is held in the change proposal and hence it is not necessary to modify the requirement's status. Another group takes the view that when it has been decided that a change proposal will be incorporated, this means that the requirement is subject to change and this indicates that its review status has changed. (This is the view taken in Chapter 2.) Whatever position is adopted, it is necessary to decide on the status values for change proposals and whether these have any impact on the review status of the affected requirements.

In summary, Acquisition organisations are mainly concerned with the creation of stakeholder requirements. This is a creative process that is difficult to scope initially. However, as the work progresses and the numbers of stakeholders and scenarios are agreed, it is possible to plan more accurately.

Change control starts off with little formality, but this evolves as the project matures through development, manufacture and in-service operation.

8.4 Supplier Organisations

Supplier organisations respond to requests from customers to build systems or components for systems. Prior to obtaining a contract to build a system, they must prepare a proposal to indicate how they intend to go about the job and containing estimates of cost and time to complete the work. Often proposals are requested from a number of supplier organisations that compete to get the business. It is therefore useful to consider supplier organisations from two points of view: bidding for work and executing a contract once the work has been won.

8.4.1 Bid Management

This section looks at the management aspects of the process to create a proposal in response to a customer's set of requirements

8.4.1.1 Planning

Often the starting point for requirements management within a supplier organisation will be the receipt of an Invitation to Tender (ITT), also known as a Request for Proposal (RFP). Such an invitation or request will contain a set of requirements that must be satisfied by the system to be delivered.

The nature of the requirements received will depend upon the organisation type of the customer (i.e. the organisation that issued the invitation). If the customer is an acquisition organisation it is likely that the requirements may be stakeholder requirements. Alternatively, the customer may be another supplier organisation that is planning to sub-contract one or more subsystems in a higher level system. In this case the requirements are likely to be system requirements with imposed design constraints. To make the narrative clearer we shall refer to the requirements received by a supplier as Input Requirements irrespective of what they really are.

Whatever the nature of the input requirements received, the first task is to assess them to determine whether they are:

- Clearly identified and distinguished from purely descriptive information
- Unambiguous
- Consistent
- Free from undue design constraints

In short, it is to determine whether they form a sound basis upon which to bid.

From a planning point of view, it is important to identify the number of requirements that must be satisfied. This provides a metric that can be used to get an idea of the scope of the work to be done.

During the review of the input requirements, any problems must be highlighted by identifying specific problems and proposing a potential solution for them. Such solutions may involve suggesting alternative wording for the requirements, or even alternative requirements that can be satisfied – perhaps with off-the-shelf components.

Once the review has been undertaken, the problems it identifies must be addressed. This will usually involve entering a dialogue with the customer to obtain clarification or authorisation for a proposed change. The extent of this dialogue will depend upon the conditions attached to the invitation. If the invitation is to a single supplier the dialogue can be entered into immediately.

However, if the invitation comes as part of a competitive bid it may be necessary to be more circumspect. The reason for this is that, usually the competition rules insist that any queries from one potential supplier are copied (together with the customer's response) to all the other potential suppliers. Hence, it is possible that, by asking questions, one supplier can give information to the other competing suppliers. In this situation, it may be more appropriate to flag the problems and observations, but rather than going back to the customer with them, discuss them internally and decide how to handle them. Possible options for each problem include:

- Ignore it.
- Make an assumption and document it.
- Decide that it is essential to ask the customer whatever the consequences.

The last action may lead to a further action to formulate the request to the customer in such a way that the competitors are helped least.

In parallel with sorting out the Input Requirements, work must proceed on creating a proposed solution. Obviously the primary output from this work is the proposal ready to be submitted to the customer. There are many different approaches to the creation of a proposal, but they all involve ensuring that each input requirement is properly addressed. The bid manager must allocate each requirement to an individual or team who will be responsible for creating a response.

It is vital that all these responses be coherent, otherwise the proposal could end up proposing a random and disconnected set of bits and pieces. The best way of achieving this is to create a model that can form the basis for the solution. Depending on the nature of the proposal, this could be either an abstract model that can form the basis for building a set of system requirements, or it can be an outline design architecture. Each response to an input requirement can then be related to the model. This provides traceability from the input requirements and it provides the coherence so that inconsistencies can be identified. The problem is always that the people working on the solution must work with incomplete information based on documented assumptions and potentially best guesses at what the customer really meant. However, this is life!

At the end of the bid phase, when the proposal has been submitted, it is important that the bid team record all the information they have accumulated during the bid preparation. The bid team will quite often be under extreme pressure to finalise and submit the bid by the required submission date. Often, they will be ready to take a break and may forget to properly record all the information in a form that can be used by the development team later. For large proposals the amount of information can be significant and also the delay between submitting the proposal and starting development can be long (e.g. 6–8 months). In these circumstances it is even more important that information is recorded, because the development team may not have any people who were involved in the bid preparation, and even if it does, after a significant period of time, they are likely to have forgotten some of the key assumptions and rationales.

A further important activity during the bid phase is the setting up of agreements with suppliers. These will usually be made conditional on the bid being successful, but they will have an impact on the level of detail to which the solution is developed. The basis of an agreement between a supplier organisation and its suppliers must be founded on a set of requirements for the components to be supplied. The level of detail that is required during the bid phase will be set by agreement between the organisations involved. This will depend upon the nature of the working relationship that exists between the organisations and the degree of experience and trust that exists. (See Agreement Process in the Generic Process introduced in Chapter 2.)

8.4.1.2 Monitoring

Measuring progress during the creation of a proposal is vital, because timescales are usually quite constrained and the submission date is not negotiable. The end point must be that the proposal clearly indicates how each input requirement will be met. However, merely asserting how a requirement will be met is not sufficient. It is also necessary to check that all the assertions are valid. This is an aspect of the review process, but an indication of progress can be obtained by comparing the percentage of input requirements that have been traced to the solution model (and hence to either system requirements or design components).

A measure of the amount of outstanding work to be done can be obtained by assessing the number of input requirements that still have outstanding problems logged against them together with the number of input requirements that still have no proposed solution.

Another important milestone in the development of a solution is the creation of a model that the team are content with. Ensuring that such a model is produced quickly and that there is "buy in" is a crucial task for the manager.

In addition to all of these monitoring devices, a measure of the quality of the system requirements must also be made. This can be done in a similar manner to that described above for acquisition organisations monitoring the creation of stakeholder requirements, by defining states and linking the progression through those states to review criteria.

8.4.1.3   Changes

During the preparation of a proposal there are three potential sources of change:

- Customer
- Suppliers
- Internal

One might think that there would be no customer changes during the preparation of a proposal, and ideally this would be true. However, it is safest not to assume this. Typically the probability of change is roughly proportional to the size of the system (or component) to be developed. For very large systems, suppliers often commence their bidding activities with an early draft of an RFP in order to get the bid team running and thinking along the right lines. Later versions are issued at intervals and may contain significant changes.

The first task on receipt of a new version of the RFP (or its requirements) is to determine the nature and extent of the changes. Depending on the customer and the medium used to issue the RFP, the location of the changes may be highlighted or completely unknown. Once found, the changes must be related to the work already done and an assessment made of the new work and rework that is now necessary.

Changes from customers can also come via responses to queries from bidders. These are usually well focussed and can be assessed quite readily.

Changes instigated by suppliers are more likely. These may be in response to an initial request for a proposal to indicate that they cannot meet the requirements as defined, or the changes may come later in the process when the supplier discovers that what was originally thought to be possible turns out not to be.

Internal changes arise for much the same reasons as the suppliers' changes. Initial assumptions turn out to be invalid and therefore an alternative approach must be taken.

Whatever the source of the change, it is essential that the various requirements baselines are kept up-to-date, i.e.:

- Input requirements
- Requirements placed on suppliers
- Assumptions and interpretations made within the bid team

8.4.2 Development

8.4.2.1 Planning

The development stage of a project commences with an agreed contract based on the proposal submitted to the customer and modified during contract negotiations. In addition to this there will be other information generated during the bidding process, but not necessarily incorporated into the proposal. This may include detailed requirements, assumptions, outline or detailed design information and an initial assessment of the risks involved in undertaking the development. This information will have been used to arrive at the estimated time and cost of the work.

The activities involved in the development stage have to be more considered and in much more detail than those at the proposal preparation or bidding stage. One important difference is that instead of producing a proposal, the proposal previously submitted may now be part of the input requirements.

The information generated during development activities will depend upon the nature of the development but will inevitably include the creation of a solution model. This may be done in two stages, firstly producing an abstract model and secondly producing one or more potential design solutions. If more than one solution is created, then it will be necessary to define the criteria for making a comparative assessment of the solutions and then deciding which one to take forward. This comparative assessment leads to the creation of options and the possibility of trading off some requirements against others. This trade off may be done entirely internal to the supplier organisation or it may involve the customer and/or the suppliers.

Activities are necessary to ensure that all the input requirements in the contractual specification are addressed, that the proposed solution embodied in the system requirements and design is adequate. The level of detail will usually have to be improved to ensure that, at the most detailed level, nothing is left to chance.

During the development stage it is important to ensure that the means of testing (or otherwise demonstrating the satisfaction of) each requirement is understood and documented.

The first step is to undertake an audit of the available information to determine its extent and quality. Ideally all the information created by the bid team should have been collected together and archived ready for use in the development process. All too frequently this is not the case and significant information can be lost. This can cause a major discontinuity between the intentions of the bid team and what is actually done by the development team. This, in turn, can put the organisation's business at risk.

Following the audit the project manager must determine, by comparing the proposal submitted with the contract, what has changed since the proposal was submitted.

The next step is to determine what the impact of these changes will be and to plan activities to make any consequential changes to the system requirements, design and component specifications.

Any outstanding assumptions and comments must be referred back to the customer, although ideally these will have been addressed during the negotiation of the contract.

A further issue that often arises when planning a development is whether the system will be delivered with full functionality at once, or whether there will be a series of releases with increasing functionality culminating with the final complete release. Supplying a series of releases provides the customer with an initial capability early. This approach is very popular in software development where there may be some doubts about the usability of the system.

From a requirements management point of view, releases must be planned on the basis of the set of requirements that will be implemented in each release. These decisions can be recorded by adding a release attribute to each requirement. Such attributes can either be enumerated lists or Boolean. A set of possible values for an enumeration list would be:

{TBD, Release 1, Release 2, Release 3}

(Where TBD stands for "To Be Decided" and will usually be the default value).

When using Boolean attributes each has the value True or False and one is created for each release.

8.4.2.2 Monitoring

Monitoring progress during the development should be focussed on assessing the current extent and quality of the output information to be generated. It is also vital to know how much time and effort has been consumed. From this knowledge it is possible to estimate whether the outputs will be complete within the effort and time allowed in the plan. This estimate must take into account the manager's knowledge of when or at what rate the information outputs are expected to be achieved.

If the manager discovers that progress is lagging behind the plan, then appropriate corrective actions can be taken. These will inevitably lead to a change in the plan, such as adjusting the duration or resources of existing activities, or adding extra activities.

The monitoring activities must ensure that project information is up-to-date. It is especially important that input requirements and supplier requirements are modified in line with agreed changes and that traceability links exist from input requirements through to supplier requirements via the proposed solution.

8.4.2.3 Changes

The same three sources of changes arise in the development as already identified in the bidding stage. The extent of customer changes is likely to be far less during development than during bidding. Internal and supplier changes are just as likely. The procedure for identifying the nature and consequence of any change is just the same. However, the consequence of a change at this point is far more serious. Small changes can be accommodated within the customer contract or supplier agreement. However, more serious changes may require a change to the terms and conditions of either. Changes introduced during development will usually have an impact on both the time scale (schedule) of the development and the cost. Once the consequences have been determined, it is then a commercial decision whether to absorb any cost and time penalties or whether to negotiate with the customer and/or suppliers.

When a change is proposed for a development with several releases, it is a function of change management to decide which release the change will be implemented in.

In summary, Supplier organisations respond to customer requests by preparing a proposal and if successful they go on to develop a system. Making sure that the requirements issued by the customer are a sound basis for the development is of prime importance. Keeping the input requirements up-to-date as changes are introduced ensures that the project is soundly based. Traceability from the input requirements to the proposed solution, to their suppliers' requirements and to testing information ensures that the impact of change can be assessed and that the organisation at all times knows the status of the development.

8.5 Product Organisations

Product organisations define stakeholder requirements and develop a product to satisfy them. Thus they have many of the characteristics of Acquisition and Supplier organisations. The main difference is that the customer–supplier agreement at the top level of the supply chain is within the overall organisation, although different departments usually undertake the roles of defining stakeholder requirements and developing products to satisfy them.

8.5.1 Planning

8.5.1.1 Single Product Version

Planning for a single version of a single product involves the same activities as for the acquisition and the supplier organisations. The difference between the bidding and the development stages may still be there. For example, when starting a new product, the company may want to have an initial idea of what is involved in building it. To achieve this it is necessary to elicit the stakeholder requirements and to produce an outline solution.

Producing the stakeholder requirements is very similar to the way in which acquisition organisations do it. There is a need to identify stakeholders and user scenarios. However, rather than interviewing real stakeholders, what usually happens is that people volunteer (or are volunteered) to act as "surrogate" stakeholders. This means that they adopt the role of a defined stakeholder and define, from that point of view, what the stakeholder requirements are. From a planning point of view there is little difference. People must still be identified and interviewed. Requirements must be extracted, properly formulated and embodied in an agreed structure. Finally the requirements must be reviewed and their quality established.

Producing an outline solution is very similar to the work done when creating a proposal. The main difference is that there is direct access to the people who are formulating the requirements and hence there is the possibility of a much more interactive development where the stakeholder requirements can be modified to make implementation easier, to reduce time to market and to reduce cost. It is even possible that the capability of a proposed product can be enhanced within the given budget by feeding back technical possibilities to the owners of the stakeholder requirements. It is clearly much easier to gain clarification where requirements are vague or confusing, etc. This may sound very informal, and in some cases, it can be. However, the degree of formality must be agreed prior to starting the work.

When an agreed set of stakeholder requirements and an outline solution have been produced and reviewed by the product organisation, it may decide not to proceed with the development or it may decide to invest further funds and go to a more detailed design or even to produce an early prototype. Thus it can be seen that a product can proceed by means of a set of stages where each stage builds upon previous work. Each stage has a given budget and a set of objectives. At the end of each stage there is a review at which progress against the budget and the objectives is assessed. This procedure can be described using the stage gate concept as indicated in Fig. 8.4.

At the initial gate (Stage Gate 0), a set of objectives, budget and timescale are defined. These feed into a planning process which determines the information which must be generated in order to achieve the stage's objectives and a work plan which will achieve the required state within the budget. The initial objective may be merely an exploration of the concept and some preliminary estimation of market size, etc. At the end of the stage the work done is reviewed against the objectives to determine whether the project should continue or whether it should stop. This review should also take into account the current business objectives, which may have changed or evolved during the stage.

If the project is allowed to continue then a further budget, timescale and objectives will be agreed. For the second stage it may be decided to go for a costed proposal as discussed above and a more detailed exploration of market conditions. The stage gate review will then check whether the estimated cost is in line with the expected revenue that can be earned. This leads naturally into a decision to cancel or commit further funds. If the latter, then a decision has to be taken about how far the development should be taken, e.g.

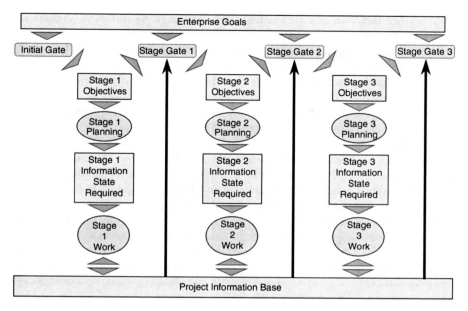

Fig. 8.4 Stage gates and project work

- Do more investigation into the development and production costs.
- Develop a prototype.
- Produce a small batch and try them out with real customers.
- Go into full production.
- Etc.

Thus the stage gate process can continue one stage at a time with gradual commitment of funds and resources. This enables the organisation to control its investment strategy and keep an eye on its likely return on investment.

8.5.1.2 Multiple Products and Versions

Product organisations may have several versions of the same product at different stages in their evolution. Typically they will have some product versions in use by people who have purchased them, some in development and some being defined. From a planning point of view, each version can be treated as a separate "project" going through its own set of stages and gates. However, there is an additional need to plan for the different versions of the products in the pipeline. It is important to plan when each version in current use will be phased out and replaced by a later model. These aspects can also be brought under the stage gate process, so that a set of stage gate reviews can be held at the same time to determine the best investment strategy to keep or increase market share.

A further factor in this area is that there may well be different versions for different markets. For example, it may be necessary to have user interfaces that support different natural languages for sale in different countries.

To cope with this type of difference we introduce the notion of a "Variant" meaning "differing in form or details from the main one". Thus we can have the "main one" (perhaps better expressed as the "core product") being a product with the user interface in English and variants for the French, German and Spanish markets. Each variant can have its own versions such that each version is an improvement over the previous one.

Figure 8.5 indicates how there can be parallel versions and variants of a single product each at a different stage of its evolution. The letters S, D and U indicate whether a product is being specified, being developed or being used. Each of these states corresponds to one or more stages in the stage gate lifecycle.

From a requirements management point of view, each variant will have many requirements in common with the core product, but it will have some requirements that are specific to that variant and therefore differentiate it from other variants. On the other hand, there may be no different requirements for each version of a variant, because each version is an attempt to satisfy the same set of requirements (hopefully improving as the sequence goes on).

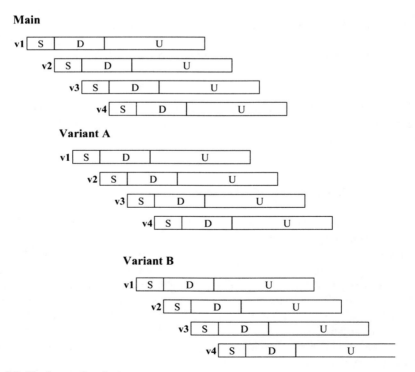

Fig. 8.5 Versions and variants

In the previous section we used the term "release" and readers may be confused between a release and a version. The difference is that a release is a version that is delivered to the customer, whereas not all versions will be.

Planning the evolution of the variants and their versions for each product is a further organisational task that can also be controlled using the stage gate mechanism. The development for these may overlap in time and there will be a need to support at least one version of each variant whilst it is in operational use.

The activities involved in doing the specification and development are very similar to those introduced earlier for the acquisition and supplier organisations. The major difference is that, where different versions and variants of the same product exist, there is common information being used in several contexts. This complicates the management of the requirements and makes it essential to understand how the requirements baselines for each version and variant overlap.

There are two approaches commonly used. In the first, requirements are marked using an attribute, to indicate whether the requirement is a common requirement or only valid for one or more variants. In the second approach a copy of all the requirements is made and changes made to the copy for a specific product variant.

An alternative approach that is gaining popularity in some organisations is to introduce an additional layer of abstraction referred to as a Feature Variability Model. Features can be used in several products and tend to be quite stable. Requirements are marked as either common or related to one or more specific features. The advantage of this approach is that, once a new feature has had its requirements introduced and marked, that feature can be used in any number of new products. Thus development effort is only required when a new feature is added to the product set, rather than work being necessary for every new product.

From a planning and organisational point of view, the introduction of a feature variability model provides a level of abstraction that product planners and marketing people can relate to. This helps focus the organisation's senior management and make them more aware of the extent and capabilities of their product portfolio.

Whichever approach is adopted, the fact that there are common requirements and variant requirements leads to extra complications in the management of change (see below).

8.5.2 Monitoring

Monitoring progress in a product organisation uses exactly the same mechanisms as for the other organisations. When stage gates are used as the basis for organisational decisions, the process of planning will involve the identification of the data state that must exist at the end of the stage. Progress can then be measured based on the extent to which the desired state has been reached. As a general rule such states can be measured in the following terms:

• Whether new objects exist that will become targets for traceability links (e.g. solution objects in response to stakeholder requirements, or design objects in response to system requirements)

- Whether attribute values exist
- Whether the required review status exists
- Whether traceability links exist from one data set to others (e.g. from stakeholder requirements to system requirements, from system requirements to design and from all of these to testing strategies and possibly test results)

Measures expressed as a percentage of required data quality currently achieved provide useful metrics for both quality of data and progress within a stage.

8.5.3 Changes

As mentioned earlier the major additional factor for change management in a product organisation is where several variants of a product have common requirements, and a change proposal is raised against one or more of them. The questions that must be answered are:

- Will all the variants want to incorporate the change?
- When will they want to incorporate it?

Quite often the answer will be that all variants will want to incorporate the change, but not at the same time! This introduces an extra state into the change handling state transition diagram (see Fig. 8.6) because each variant must incorporate the change before the change can be completed.

Figure 8.6 also indicates that it is necessary that there are Planned, Deferred and Incorporated states for each variant. The change can only achieve the status of complete when all the variants have reached their individual 'Incorporated' state.

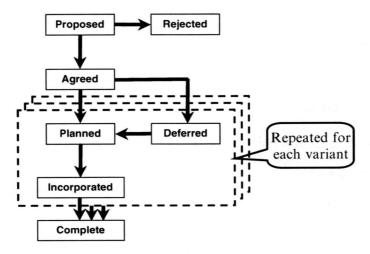

Fig. 8.6 Modified STD for change management with variants

In summary, Product organisations perform similar tasks to both Acquisition and Supplier organisations. In addition they must take care to control their product portfolio so that an appropriate degree of commitment is made and the overall commercial exposure is acceptable.

8.6 Summary

The summary is grouped under the headings of planning, monitoring and changes in line with the presentation of the main body of the text.

8.6.1 Planning

Planning should be driven by the outputs that must be created. Activities to create the required outputs can then be introduced. Outputs can be categorised as follows:

- Types of information objects (e.g. stakeholders, stakeholder requirements, system requirements, design or solution objects, etc.).
- Attributes associated with an information object.
- Links between information objects to establish traceability, testing strategy, etc.
- Review criteria to determine the required quality of information and associated attributes.
- Achievement of a particular state possibly via progression through a series of states (e.g. by reviews).

Before any work can be started, the work must be authorised by the organisation in which it will be undertaken. A mechanism such as stage gates is appropriate for Acquisition and Product organisations to control the level of commitment and consequent financial and/or commercial exposure they are willing to tolerate. In Supplier organisations there must be an authorisation to prepare a proposal and this is usually accompanied by an allowed budget. Permission to progress to development will usually be embodied in the signing of a contract with the customer.

Evolutionary development should be considered to be the norm especially for unprecedented systems. This leads naturally into the concepts of releases, versions and variants.

8.6.2 Monitoring

It is vital that progress is measured by investigating the current state of the required outputs. Progress measured in this way together with the amount of effort and time used compared to the plan enables the viability of the plan to be established. Ignoring the outputs and just measuring time and effort consumed gives a distorted view that is not realistic.

8.6.3 Changes

The most critical aspect of a change is the impact that it will have on the system to be developed and hence on the development plan. Understanding the impact can only be achieved provided that the current states of the (project) outputs are available and up-to-date. Of particular importance here are the links that exist to provide traceability from input information to derived information.

Deciding when a change can or should be incorporated will usually impact the plan and may cause serious re-planning – depending on the scope of the change. Changes can also lead to the introduction of additional releases, version or variants.

Chapter 9
DOORS: A Tool to Manage Requirements

There's nothing remarkable about it.
All one has to do is hit the right keys at the right time
and the instrument plays itself.

Johann Sebastian Bach, composer, 1685–1750 AD

9.1 Introduction

Systems engineers and managers need the right instruments to assist them with the requirements management process. A variety of tools currently exist. This chapter presents an overview of one of these tools – IBM Rational® DOORS® (Version 9.2). DOORS (Dynamic Object Oriented Requirements System) is a leading requirements management tool used by tens of thousands of engineers around the world. The tool was originally created by QSS Ltd, Oxford and is now developed and marketed by IBM.

DOORS is a multi-platform, enterprise-wide requirements management tool designed to capture, link, trace, analyse and manage a wide range of information to ensure a project's compliance to specified requirements and standards. DOORS provides for the communication of business needs, allows cross-functional teams to collaborate on development projects to meet these needs, and enables you to validate that the right system is being built, and is being built right. The views provided by DOORS on the screen provide a powerful familiar navigation mechanism.

Also briefly covered in this chapter is a DOORS extension called DOORS/Analyst, which integrates DOORS with the IBM Rational® Tau® modelling tool, allowing UML models to be embedded and traced within DOORS.

Throughout this chapter reference will be made to a case study for a family sailing boat. The DOORS/Analyst discussion uses part of a case study for an airport baggage handling system.

E. Hull et al., *Requirements Engineering*, DOI 10.1007/978-1-84996-405-0_9,
© Springer-Verlag London Limited 2011

9.2   The Case for Requirements Management

Today, systems engineers require effective requirements management in order to provide solutions. Requirements management is the process that captures, traces and manages stakeholder needs and the changes that occur throughout a project's lifecycle. Products, too, are becoming more complex to the point where no individual has the ability to comprehend the whole, nor understand all of its constituent parts. Structuring is by far the best way of organising requirements, thus making them more manageable in terms of omissions or duplicate information. Hence requirements management is also about communication. For that reason it is important that requirements are communicated correctly, thus ensuring that team collaboration is enhanced, project risk is reduced and the project meets its business objectives. If requirements are well managed, the right product will get to market on time, on budget and to specification.

9.3   DOORS Architecture

For any application, the requirements and related information can be stored in a central database in DOORS. This database can be accessed in a variety of ways and exists throughout the lifetime of the application. The information in a DOORS database is stored in modules. Modules can be organised within the database by using folders and projects. A project is a special kind of folder that contains all the data for a particular project (Fig. 9.1).

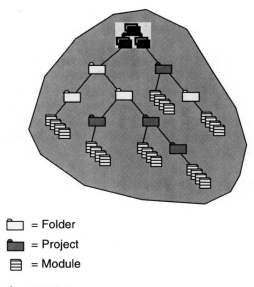

☐ = Folder
▰ = Project
☰ = Module

Fig. 9.1   DOORS database structure

DOORS *folders* are used to organise data and are just like folders in a computer file store. Folders may contain other folders, projects or modules. Folders are given a name and description and the ability for users to see or manipulate the data in a folder may be constrained using access controls.

DOORS *projects* are used by a team of people to manage a collection of data relating to that team's work effort. The project should contain all of the data related to the requirements, design, development, test, production and maintenance for an application. The project provides the capability to manage users and their access to the data in the project, to back-up the data and to distribute portions of the data to other DOORS databases.

DOORS *modules* are containers for data sets. Three classes of module exist:

- *Formal* – the most frequently used type of module for structured sets of like information.
- *Descriptive* – unstructured source information (letters or interview notes).
- *Link* – contain relationships between other data elements.

The user interface works very much like Windows Explorer and lets the user navigate through the database.

9.4 Projects, Modules and Objects

9.4.1 DOORS Database Window

The DOORS Database window allows the user to see and manage the organisation of DOORS data. Figure 9.2 shows the database window, with the database explorer to the left, and the list of contents of the selected folder on the right.

DOORS provides the capability to change the name or description of existing folders and projects. Folders and projects can also be moved if there is a need to reorganise or change the structure of the database. Folders and projects can also be cut, copied or pasted within the database to reorganise or duplicate portions of the database.

9.4.2 Formal Modules

Using the DOORS Database window, a new formal module can be created using the menu **File ▶ New ▶ Formal Module** as shown in Fig. 9.3.

In the formal module creation window, the user provides the name of the new module and its description. The user can also determine the starting point for the unique identifiers generated for the objects in the module. A prefix can be provided for this number that reflects the contents of the module, such as PR for Product Requirements. By defining a unique prefix for each module, a project-wide unique

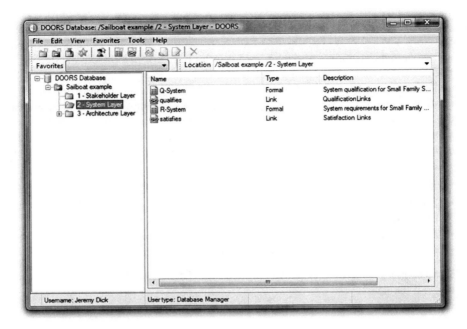

Fig. 9.2 Database window

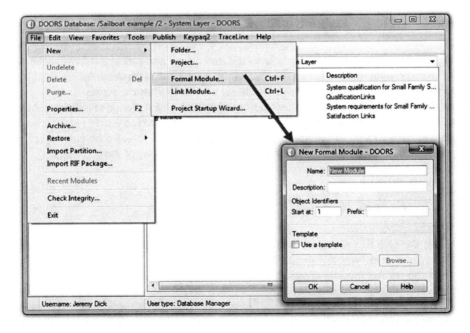

Fig. 9.3 Create new formal module

identifier for all information in the DOORS project is established. This provides a convenient reference.

When a formal module is opened, the default display shows the module explorer on the left, and the module data on the right as shown in Fig. 9.4.

The module explorer makes it easy to move to a specific place in the document, and also shows the structure of the information in the module. Sections can be expanded or collapsed in the same way as can be done with Windows Explorer.

The right hand pane shows the data for the module. The default display shows two columns, the "ID" column and the "text" column, whose title is the module description. The ID is a unique identifier assigned by DOORS when an object is created. DOORS uses this identifier to keep track of the object and any other information that is associated with it, e.g. attributes and links. The text column displays the data like a document, showing a combination of the heading number, the heading itself and the text associated with each the requirement.

DOORS provides a number of display options for formal modules as shown in Fig. 9.5. In the *Standard View*, all levels of objects are displayed in a 'document' format. Users can restrict the display level, e.g. *Outline* displays only headings, hiding all other object details. This result is similar to a typical document 'table of contents'. As stated earlier the *Explorer View* is useful for seeing the structure of the module and for navigating to a specific object in the module.

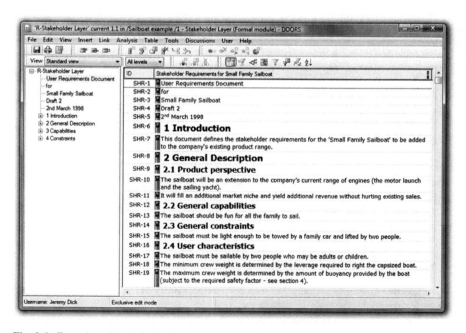

Fig. 9.4 Formal module default display

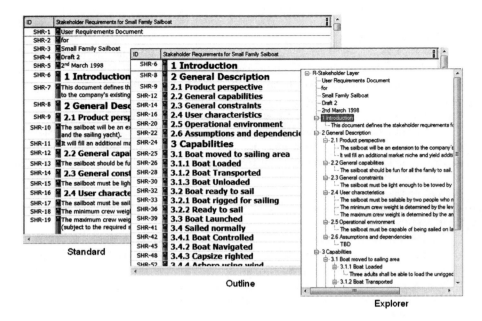

Fig. 9.5 Formal module display modes

Graphics mode on the other hand represents the display as a tree. This aids navigation through large data sets. The titles of the objects in graphics mode are based on the *Object Heading* and a shortened version of the *Object Text* (see Fig. 9.6).

9.4.3 Objects

As we have seen in the previous section, within formal modules, data is stored in objects. An object may be a block of text, a graphic image or even a spreadsheet created using another package. The standard view of a formal module display includes two columns and a number of visual indicators as described below.

As shown in Fig. 9.7 the first column displays the *Object Identifier* assigned by DOORS. The Object Identifier is made up of two parts:

- A prefix (typically an abbreviation for the requirement set).
- The absolute number, supplied by DOORS.

The absolute number is an integer assigned sequentially (1, 2, 3 etc.) that serves as a key for each object, unique within the module.

The second column is known as the *Main* or *Text* column. It includes a composite three attributes, depending on contents:

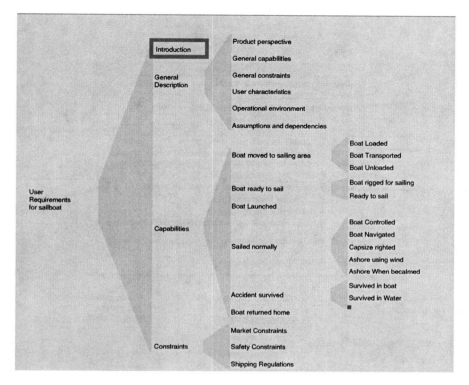

Fig. 9.6 Graphics mode

- Section number (e.g. 1, 2.1, 3.2.3) indicating the object's position in the module structure.
- Object heading providing a title for the object.
- Object text giving the full description of the object.

Object numbers are only displayed for objects that have been assigned an object heading.

Black lines above and below the object indicate the Current Object. Many functions relating to objects in DOORS modules, e.g. inserting a new object, pasting an object and moving an object are performed relative to the current object.

Blue, yellow and red *change bars* appear at the left edge of the text column. Blue denotes an object that has not been changed since the last module baseline. Yellow shows that changes have been saved since the baseline and red indicates unsaved changes made in the current session.

Maroon and orange *link indicators* are displayed on the right hand side of objects, which have relationships to other objects. The orange triangle pointing to the left indicates an incoming link, and a maroon triangle pointing to the right indicates an outgoing link (only incoming indicators are present in Fig. 9.7).

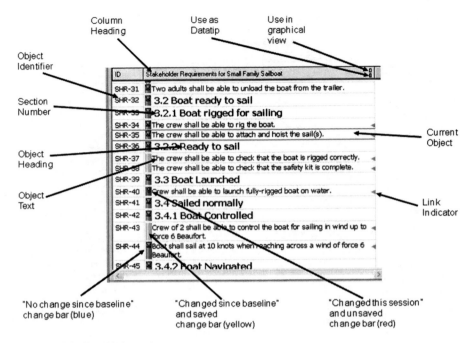

Fig. 9.7 Displayed information

A DOORS formal module tree structure provides a simple, yet powerful method of writing requirements. Requirements are often organised into a hierarchy, and so the graphics mode is a useful view.

Creating new objects in DOORS is simple – new objects are placed in one of two positions relative to the current object. Either:

- A new object is created as the next sibling of the current object with **Insert ▶ Object**, or
- An object is created as the first child below the current object with **Insert ▶ Object Below**.

This is shown in Fig. 9.8.

In DOORS, facilities are provided for editing objects. For example, a DOORS tree can be modified by using the cut and paste functions. The *Cut* operation removes the current object and all its children from the module display. This causes the rearrangement of the object hierarchy, collapsing the tree into the hole vacated by the objects that have been cut. This produces a renumbering of the remaining successor objects. The insertion point can then be identified for the objects that have been cut. Because of the nature of an object hierarchy there are only two possibilities. Objects are placed *after* as the next sibling to the current object or one level down as the first child of the current object. The former is shown in Fig. 9.9.

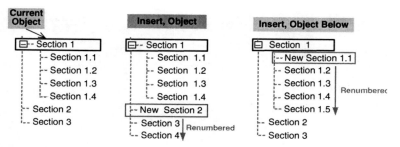

Fig. 9.8 Creating objects

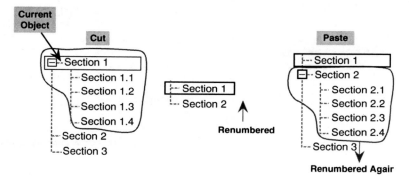

Fig. 9.9 Cut and paste objects

9.4.4 *Graphical Objects*

Graphical objects in the form of embedded OLEs can be inserted into any text attribute in DOORS, in much the same way as OLEs are handled in Word, for instance. This allows pictures, diagrams, charts, documents, spreadsheets, and many other kinds of information to be inserted into the requirements document in support of requirements statements.

9.4.5 *Tables*

In many cases, requirements or information associated with requirements is presented in tabular form. Tables can be created after or below an existing object, or at level one in an empty module. This is achieved by specifying the number of rows and columns required. The new table can then be inserted into the formal module as shown in Fig. 9.10. Tables can be deleted as long as there are no links to any of the cell objects or to the table object.

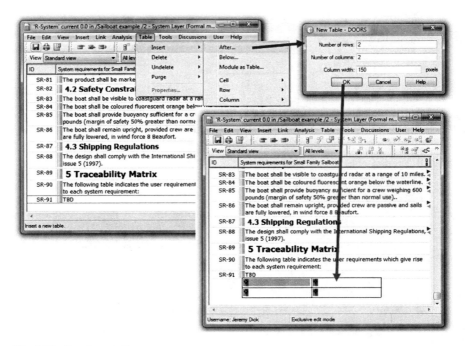

Fig. 9.10 Creating a table

9.5 History and Version Control

9.5.1 History

DOORS maintains an historical log of all module and object level actions that modify the contents of a module, its objects and attributes.

Every change that is recorded includes who made the change, when the change was made and what were the before/after states of the object and its attributes. The module history can be used to track every event in the life of a given module. The object history can be accessed via the change bar in the formal module window or it can be launched from the main menu. An example history window is shown in Fig. 9.11.

9.5.2 Baselining

A baseline is a frozen copy of a module. They are typically created at significant stages of a project, e.g. a set of requirements is normally baselined immediately prior to a review, and then immediately after the resulting changes from the review have been incorporated. This allows the various states of the requirements document to be easily reproduced at any time. Baselines can be numbered and labelled in DOORS.

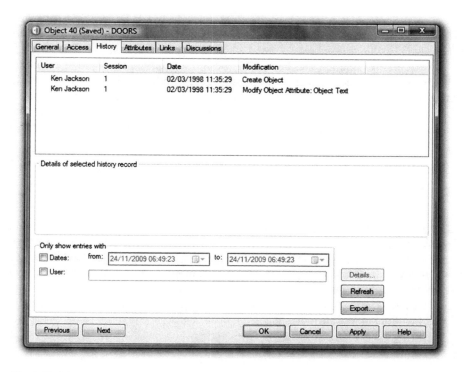

Fig. 9.11 History window

Baselines are read-only copies of a formal module and cannot be edited. When a module is baselined, all history since the previous baseline is stored with the newly created baseline, and the history for the current version is cleared. The life history of a module is therefore stored across a series of baselines.

9.6 Attributes and Views

9.6.1 Attributes

Attributes provide a means to annotate modules and objects with related information. Module attributes are used to capture information about the module itself, such as its owner, document control number, review states etc. Object attributes are used to capture information about individual objects. Attributes may be either system- or user-defined. System attributes automatically maintain critical information about a module or object, such as when it was created and by whom, while user-defined attributes may be used to capture any information required to support the user's requirements management process.

DOORS provides a variety of standard attribute types, known as *base types*, from which attributes may be defined, e.g. integer, real, date, string, text, user name. It is also possible to have user defined attribute types.

Attribute information can be readily viewed and edited by creating columns. In this way, on-screen as well as printable reports can be readily generated. While an object may contain many attributes, a user is typically interested in viewing a subset of these attributes at one time. Columns may be created to show just the desired subset so that the user is not overwhelmed with information. Simply dragging and dropping the column header can reposition columns.

9.6.2 Views

DOORS provides a facility called *views* for looking at the same information in many different ways. Views are stored with modules and it is possible to create many views from a project's data. When creating views the object and attributes which are to be displayed are specified. For example, you might wish to create a view that lets you see only those objects in the module whose 'Priority' attribute has a value 'High'. A view then appears as a table, where each row contains one object and the object attributes that have been selected.

9.7 Traceability

Traceability is managed in DOORS through the use of links between objects.

9.7.1 Links

A DOORS link is a connection between two objects. One property of a link is directionality; all links have a direction, from source to target. To represent data relationships a link is created, thus enabling the user to visualize information as a network rather than just a tree. Although links have directionality, DOORS provides the capability to navigate in either direction through the path that a link creates between two objects. Hence it is possible to trace the impact of changes in one document on another document, or trace backwards to indicate the original thinking behind a decision.

DOORS provides a variety of methods for creating and maintaining links. Individual links can be created using drag-and-drop between two objects (usually in different modules). Whole sets of links can be created in other ways. For instance, the *Copy and link* function can copy a whole set of objects, and link each copy to its original.

Links are indicated along the right hand side of the main column in the standard view of a formal module by triangular link icons. An icon that points to the left represents incoming links; the opposite for outgoing links.

9.7.2 Traceability Reports

There are a number of ways in DOORS of creating traceability reports, on screen and on paper. The simplest on-screen traceability tool is through using **Analysis ▶ Traceability Explorer**, which uses a Windows-style interface to allow the user to explore traceability across multiple documents in a single window. This is illustrated in Fig. 9.12.

Another way of constructing an on-screen report (which can subsequently be printed) is by adding traceability columns to a view. These columns can display data about linked objects from other documents. They are created using **Analysis ▶ Wizard,** which guides the user to select which links and which attributes of linked objects are to be displayed. Traceability columns are completely dynamic, and are updated as new links are created, or as the distant data is changed. Through this means, data from several documents can be brought together into a single report, on-screen or printed onto paper.

Figure 9.13 shows an example of a view that contains a traceability column. The view lives in the current module, which is the Stakeholder Requirements, and the

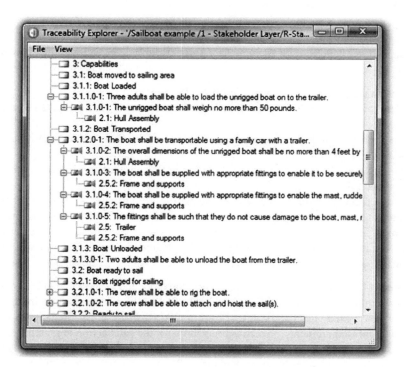

Fig. 9.12 Traceability explorer

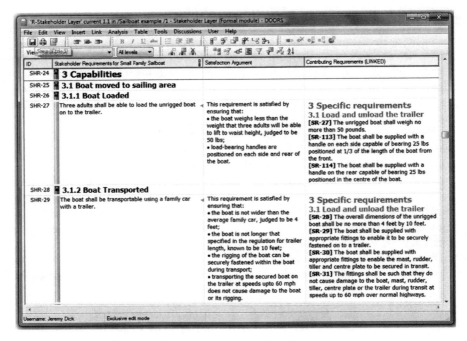

Fig. 9.13 Traceability columns showing requirments satisfaction

column shows data from the System Requirements module by following the incoming links. Rich traceability is used in the example, and the columns are as follows:

- The Stakeholder requirement identifier (from current module).
- The main column showing the Stakeholder requirement heading/text (from current module).
- The rich traceability combinator (an attribute of the Stakeholder requirement in the current module).
- The satisfaction argument (an attribute of the Stakeholder requirement in the current module).
- A traceability column entitled "Contributing Requirements" showing several attributes of system requirements linked to the stakeholder requirement. The object identifier of the system requirement is shown bold in square brackets, followed by the text. In addition, the section headings of each system requirement are shown to give essential context within the System Requirements document.

Figure 9.14 shows a traceability column from the other end of the same links, i.e. from the System Requirements document back to the Stakeholder Requirements. In this case, the outgoing links are traversed, and information is displayed in the column entitle "originating Requirements". There is no column for the satisfaction arguments.

It is common for requirements documentation to include traceability matrices showing the relationships between documents. Through the use of traceability columns in views, DOORS avoids the need to create and maintain such matrices manually.

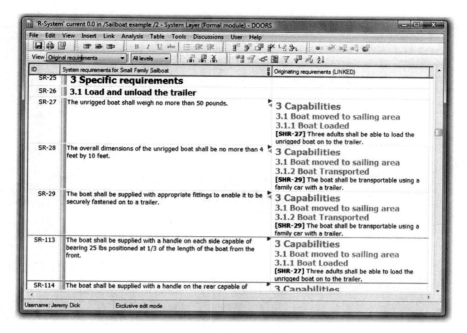

Fig. 9.14 Traceability column on outgoing links

9.8   Import and Export

The capability of exchanging information between DOORS and other tools is highly desirable. This can range from importing legacy information into DOORS and for exporting DOORS information to external tools for publishing and other purposes.

In project development the ability to efficiently and reliably import and organise large quantities of information is often a necessary task. However the variety of storage formats and platforms and the inconsistencies in data structures can make this a real challenge. DOORS provides a wide range of import tools to support this activity and in particular in relation to documents, tables and databases. For example, Fig. 9.15 shows how to input from Word into DOORS. This is achieved by opening a Word document and exporting it to DOORS, using the **Export to DOORS** button – a module name and description needs to be supplied before the file is exported from Word and imported into DOORS.

The document is imported into DOORS with the same structure as the Word Outline view, so Heading 1 text becomes an object at the level 1 in DOORS. Paragraph breaks are used for delimiting the content of each object.

Similarly, DOORS supports many export formats to provide a convenient method of transferring DOORS data to other desktop tools. As an example consider exporting from DOORS to Word as shown in Fig. 9.16.

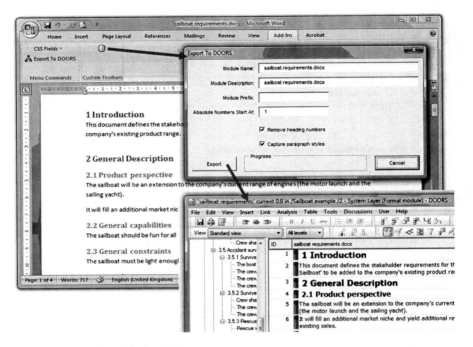

Fig. 9.15 Export from Word to DOORS

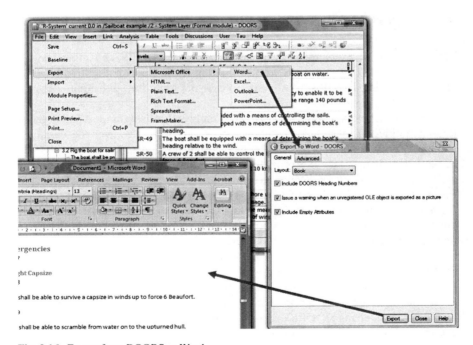

Fig. 9.16 Export from DOORS to Word

This is the reverse of the previous operation. The Word document will have the same structure as the formal module, i.e. Object Heading 1 becomes Level 1 Headings become Word style "Heading 1", and so on. Text is displayed in Normal style.

DOORS provides these types of import and export capabilities for a range of tools and formats including: RTF, Word, WordPerfect, Excel, Lotus, Access, Plain Text, HTML, PowerPoint, MS Project, Outlook and many others.

9.9 UML Modelling with DOORS/Analyst

DOORS/Analyst is an integration of DOORS with the UML modelling tool, IBM Rational® Tau®. It permits UML models to be created and diagrams to be presented within a DOORS module.

As requirements are analysed, objects in a DOORS module can be labelled as UML elements, such as actors, classes and states. When a diagram is inserted into the DOORS module by activating the UML modelling tool, the DOORS objects so labelled are synchronised with elements that appear in the diagrams. The effect of this is to allow traceability of requirements into elements that appear in diagrams in UML.

Figure 9.17 shows a screen-shot of a DOORS module in which DOORS/Analyst has been used to label objects, and insert a class diagram. Labelled objects are indicated by icons in the narrow column to the left of the main column, and the type of UML entity is also shown in the "Object Type" column to the right.

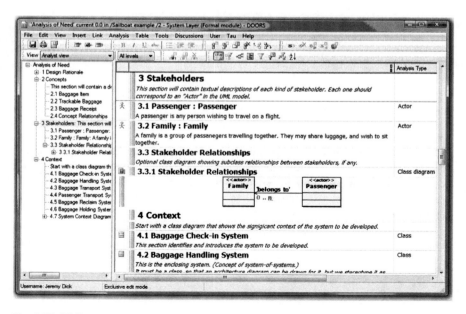

Fig. 9.17 UML modelling in DOORS/Analyst

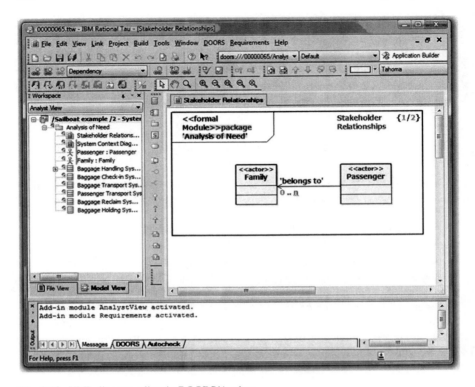

Fig. 9.18 UML diagram editor in DOORS/Analyst

Double-clicking on a diagram starts up the DOORS/Analyst diagram editor, shown in Fig. 9.18. Saving changes to the model causes information to be re-synchronised into the DOORS module.

9.10 Summary

A brief overview of a requirements management tool, DOORS, has been given in this chapter. The example used shows the application of some of the principles used in the book, e.g. instantiations of the generic process in layers, rich traceability, etc.

DOORS/Analyst is also introduced as an example of how modelling tools can compliment requirements management tools.

The same principles can be applied and implemented in other requirements management tools. Even if one is just using a word processor, the disciplines described within the covers of this book will be beneficial.

Bibliography

Alderson A, Hull MEC, Jackson K and Griffiths LE (1998) Method Engineering for Industrial Real-Time and Embedded Systems. *Information and Software Technology*, 40: 443–454.

Andriole SJ (1996) *Managing Systems Requirements: Methods, Tools and Cases.* New York, McGraw-Hill.

Babich W (1986) *Software Configuration Management – Coordination for Team Productivity.* Boston, MA, Addison-Wesley.

Bernstein P (1996) *Against the Gods – the Remarkable Story of Risk.* New York, Wiley.

Boehm B (1981) *Software Engineering Economics.* New York, Prentice-Hall.

Booch G (1994) *Object-oriented Design with Applications.* Redwood City, California, Benjamin Cummins.

Brown AW, Earl AN et al. (1992) *Software Engineering Environments.* London, McGraw-Hill.

Budgen D (1994) *Software Design.* Boston, MA, Addison-Wesley.

CarnegieMellon (2006) *Software Engineering Institute, CMMI® for Development, Version 1.2, CMMI-DEV, Pitsburg, PA 15213–3890*

Chaochen Z, Hoare CAR, Ravn AP (1991) A Calculus of Durations. *Information Processing Letter,* 40(5): 269–276.

Chen, Peter (1976) The Entity-Relationship Model – Toward a Unified View of Data. In: *ACM Transactions on Database Systems 1/1/1976.* ACM-Press, ISSN 0362-5915, S. 9–36

Clark KB and Fujimoto T (1991) *Product Development Performance.* Harvard Business School.

Coad P and Yourdon E (1991a) *Object-Oriented Analysis.* Englewood Cliffs, NJ, Prentice-Hall.

Coad P and Yourdon E (1991b) *Object-Oriented Design.* Englewood Cliffs, NJ, Prentice-Hall.

Cooper RG (1993) *Winning at New Products.* Reading, MA, Addison Wesley.

Crosby PB (1979) *Quality Is Free.* New York, McGraw-Hill.

Crosby PB (1984) *Quality Without Tears.* New York, New American Library.

Darke P, Shanks GG (1947) User Viewpoint Modelling: Understanding and Representing User Viewpoints During Requirements Definition. *Information Systems Journal* 7(3): 213–240.

Davis AM (1993) *Software Requirements: Objects, Functions and States.* Englewood Cliffs, NJ, Prentice-Hall.

DeGrace P (1993) *The Olduvai Imperative: CASE and the State of Software Engineering Practice.* Englewood Cliffs, NJ, Prentice-Hall.

DeMarco T (1978) *Structured Analysis and System Specification.* New York, Yourdon.

DeMarco T (1982) *Controlling Software Projects.* Englewood Cliffs, NJ, Yourdon Press.

DeMarco T and Lister T (1987) *Peopleware – Productive Projects and Teams.* New York, Dorset House.

Easterbrook S and Nuseibeh B (1996) Using Viewpoints for Inconsistency Management. *Software Engineering Journal,* 11(1): 31–43.

Finkelstein A, Kramer J, Nuseibeh B and Goedicke M (1992) Viewpoints: A Framework for Integrating Multiple Perspectives in Systems Development. *International Journal of Software Engineering and Knowledge Engineering,* 2(10): 31–58.

Fowler M and Scott K (1997) *UML Distilled: Applying the Standard Object Modeling Language.* Reading, MA, Addison-Wesley.

Gilb T (1988) *Principles of Software Engineering Management.* Reading, MA, Addison-Wesley.

Gilb T (2005) *Competitive Engineering: A Handbook for Systems Engineering, Requirements Engineering and Software Engineering Management Using Planguage.* Oxford, Elsevier Butterworth-Heinemann

Gorchels L (1997) *The Product Manager's Handbook.* Lincolnwood, IL, NTC Business Books.

Gotel OCZ and Finkelstein ACW (1995) Contribution Structures. *Proceedings RE'95.* York, UK, IEEE Press.

Harel D (1987) Statecharts: A Visual Formalism for Complex Systems. *Science of Computer Programming,* 8: 231–274.

Hull MEC, Taylor PS, Hanna JRP and Millar RJ (2002) Software Development Processes – An Assessment. *Information and Software Technology,* 44(1): 1–12.

Humphrey WM (1989) *Managing the Software Process.* Boston, MA, Addison-Wesley.

IEEE STD 1220–1998 (1998) *Standard for Application and Management of the Systems Engineering Process.* New York, NY, IEEE.

Jackson M (1995) Software Requirements & Specifications: a Lexicon of Practice, Principles and Prejudices. New York, NY, Addison-Wesley.

Jacobsen I and Christerson M et al (1993) *Object-Oriented Software Engineering.* Wokingham, Addison-Wesley.

Kotonya G and Sommerville I (1996) Requirements Engineering with Viewpoints. *Software Engineering Journal,* 11(1): 5–11.

Kotonya G and Sommerville I (1998) *Requirements Engineering: Processes and Techniques.* Chichester, Wiley.

Leite JCP and Freeman PA (1991) Requirements Validation Through Viewpoint Resolution. *Transactions of Software Engineering,* 12(2): 1253–1269.

Loucopulos P and Karakostas V (1995) *Systems Requirements Engineering.* New York, NY, McGraw-Hill.

Mazza C et al (1994) ESA – Software Engineering Standards. Prentice-Hall.

Monroe RT, Kompanek A, Metlon R, and Garlan D (1997) Architectural Styles, Design Patterns, and Objects. *IEEE Software.*

Mumford E (1989) User Participation in a Changing Environment – Why We Need IT. In: *Participation in Systems Development.* Ed. K Knight. London, Kogan Page.

Nuseibeh B, Kramer J and Finkelstein A (1994) A Framework for Expressing the Relationships Between Multiple Views in Requirements Specification. *Transactions of Software Engineering,* 20(10): 760–773.

Oliver DW, Kelliher TP and Keegan JG (1997) Engineering Complex Systems with Models and Objects. New York, McGraw-Hill.

OMG (2003) *The Unified Modelling Language Version 2,* www.omg.org

Page-Jones M (1980 *The Practical Guide to Structured Systems.* New York, Yourdon Press.

Perrow C (1984) *Normal Accidents.* Basic Books.

Petroski H (1982) *To Engineer is Human – the Role of Failure in Successful Design.* New York, St Martin's Press.

Petroski H (1996) *Invention by Design: How Engineers Get from Thought to Thing.* Harvard University Press.

Poots C, Takahashi K et al (1994) Inquiry-based Requirements Analysis. *IEEE Software,* 11(2): 21–32.

Pressman RS (1997) *Software Engineering: A Practitioner's Approach.* New York, NY, McGraw-Hill.

Ross DT (1977) Structured Analysis (SA): A Language for Communicating Ideas. *IEEE Transactions on Software Engineering,* 3(1): 16–34.

Ross DT (1985) Applications and Extensions of SADT. *IEEE Computer,* 18(4): 25–34.

Ross DT and Schoman KE (1977) Structured Analysis for Requirements Definition. *IEEE Transactions on Software Engineering,* 3(1): 6–15.

Rumbaugh J and Blaha M et al (1991) *Object Modeling and Design.* Englewood Cliffs, NJ, Prentice-Hall.

Rumbaugh J, Blaha M, Premerlani W, Eddy F and Lorenzen W (1991) *Object-Oriented Modeling and Design.* Prentice-Hall.

Shlaer S and Mellor SJ (1991) *Object Life Cycles – Modeling the World in States.* Yourdon Press.

Shlaer S and Mellor SJ (1998) *Object-Oriented Systems Analysis.* Englewood Cliffs NJ, Prentice-Hall.

Software Engineering Institute (Carnegie-Mellon) (1991) Capability Maturity Model for Software. Tech. Report CMU/SEI-91-TR-24.

Sommervile I (1996) *Software Engineering.* Wokingham, Addison-Wesley.

Sommervile I and Sawyer P (1997) *Requirements Engineering: A Good Practice Guide.* Chichester, Wileyons.

Spivey JM (1989) *The Z Notation: A Reference Manual.* Englewood Cliffs, NJ, Prentice-Hall.

Stevens R, Brook P, Jackson K and Arnold S (1998) *Systems Engineering: Coping with Complexity.* Prentice-Hall Europe.

Yourdon EN (1990) *Modern Structured Analysis.* Englewood Cliffs, NJ, Prentice-Hall.

Zave P (1997) Classification of Research Efforts in Requirements Engineering. *ACM Computing Surveys,* 29(4): 315–321.

Index

Lightning Source UK Ltd.
Milton Keynes UK
15 November 2010

162902UK00007B/77/P